A Safe and Brave Space

Anthology of Poetry and Art

The Mission of the Garden of Neuro Institute is to provide a space for women to find and create their own lives with voice, purpose, agency and leadership.

Women Poets and Artists in the Garden of Neuro Institute

Published by Garden of Neuro Publishing
A Division of the Garden of Neuro Institute
Poughkeepsie, New York
www.GardenofNeuroPublishing.com

ISBN NUMBER 978-1-962077-02-6
Cover Art & Design by: Pratibha Savani
Designed & Edited by: Nanci Arvizu & Pratibha Savani
Journal Page Designs by Pratibha Savani
Publishing Guidance by Lisa Tomey-Zonneveld

Thank You

Thank you my sisters, you women who have embraced me and all my weirdness. It's amazing to me that we are all here together. The world literally had to stop for our paths to cross, and a digital world to bring us together.

In this community we have found ourselves, and what it means to be whole. Even when that means many pieces, no worries, we've got the Kitsugi gold.

The glue that holds us together are our words, our stories, and our difficult truths. When we're allowed to use our voice, we finally find our groove.

As each one of us steps into our power, we have the chance to do more. The greatest work we do is to lift the next woman up, higher than before.

Where she too will become a light, along a path that will always be under construction. And we are making the plans, for all of us to create abundance and joy, and inspire the same in those around us.

To each of the women who've been a part of this project ~ and all the other noodles ~ I truly cannot thank you enough. From my heart you yours, today and always, in my Garden Sisters I Trust.

Thank you all for holding the pieces of my heart.
~ Nanci Arvizu

Invitation

I finally started watching Susan Brearley's intro videos in the Garden. Every time I run into things in the Garden, I feel like I'm encountering myself talking to myself. I know that sounds crazy, but I feel like I've heard these words before, as if they are, and always were, a part of my being.

I listened to Nanci Arvizu's intro video today.

"I'm done with this story. I will write my story and I will speak my truth but then I'm going to write myself into a new story by designing the life I want to live with the power of my words and giving them up to the universe to manifest." she said.

From what I can see, Nanci is a bright shining star of accomplishment.

I feel like the Garden is a little life raft – a raft stuffed to the brim with voices of women who want me to succeed. I don't know why they want me to succeed, but now I hear these voices when the nasty voices in my head get too loud.

These women come, gliding through dangerous waters, the strength of their arms battling the rough waves. Before I can see them, I hear them singing – like a hum that belongs to the universe.

It's a song of peace and love and strength.
I know this even though I can't make out the words.

Then I see them, distant figures silhouetted against the horizon. I am always stunned at their appearance. No matter the tumultuous weather, they arrive determined, consistent.

I feel their song and recognize it as my own, calling my heart home.

When my daughter was born, I thought she was perfect. I knew as they held her up and I saw her for the very first time, that each one of us spends our entire lives trying to return to the purity of the moment of our birth. The moment when we are still one with the universe. The moment of our perfection.

This is their song, the song of the universe. I hear you, my tribe. I am waving from the shore. I feel your courage thrumming in my blood. I am building my raft, but for now, I hope you can hear my lone voice on the shore, loud and strong joining yours.

We are the song that will change the world.

~ Rebecca Barrett

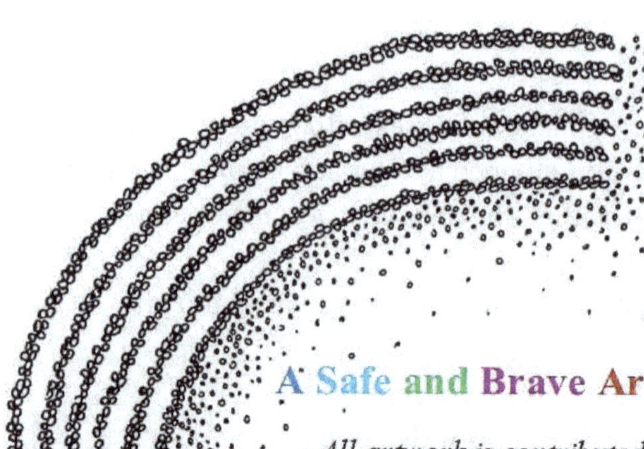

A Safe and Brave Art Space

All artwork is contributed by the
Garden of Neuro Ambassadors

Welcome to the creative spaces
in our third anthology

Our incredible garden artists have collectively
captured their safe and brave spaces utilising the
black and white mindfulness art theme in a range
of styles and techniques to satisfy our colouring
sensations. This is an interactive element that
was guided by a specially designed online
art workshop to cover the brief.

There are also plenty of journaling pages
carrying the mindfulness theme in the form
of a rainbow, for us to freely imagine, reflect,
doodle and write in creatively plus the
dedicated 7 Day Reflection tasks.

Engage in mindfulness throughout the pages
and grab your colour pens for a fully
exquisite experience.

Art and intro by Pratibha Savani

Table of Contents

Thank You iii

Invitation iv

A Safe and Brave Art Space vi

Tanja Ajtic

Safe place 1

Safe and Brave Space 2

Nanci Arvizu

Kintsugi 3

What If 4

Jurčević Katarina

Literature is feminine 6

Arlene S Bice

The Weeping Willow 9

Planned and Unplanned 10

Natalie Bisso

Stay Human 11

A Strange Age 12

The Flame of Faith 14

Yasmin S Brown

Brave and Safe Space 17

Lin Marshall Brummels

Hidden Playhouse 18

Wrong Door 19

Mantra 20

Joni Karen Caggiano

Blissful 23

River's Harmony 24

Fish a Spell 25

Vanessa Caraveo

A Flight of Hope 29

She Perseveres 30

Jeri Day

Be 33

If 33

Whisper 33

Anna Ferriero

Lunar Salt 34

Sweet Condemnation 35

Nolcha Fox

My Father's Cigars 39

Not That Hole 40

Junk in a Trunk 41

Robin Klammer

Garden of Soul Sisters 42

Lisa Hartsgrove

Apartment 5 45

In-Between Thoughts 46

Tina Hudak

Or so… 49

Poem for Hecate 50

Chyrel J. Jackson

Emeril Couldn't Burn Like Mommy 53

Silence is not an Option 55

Autumn Makes Me Long for Summertime 57

Alison Jennings

Sky Dancers (Dakini) 61

A Cry in the Dark 62

Soul Sisters (To Lisa) 63

Zaneta Varnado Johns

Healing Touch, for Staci Jackson 67

Natural State of Mind 70

Special Gift 69

Jill Sharon Kimmelman

A New Tradition 73

Barbara Leonhard

I Have Been Her Kind 79

My Mother Couldn't Nurse Me 81

Danielle Martin

Beach Vibes 85

Dipping Into the Past 86

No Matter Where You Are 87

Indy Samra

    Shielded 88

Lauren Oertel

    Passing on a Curve 91

    It's Not Too Late 93

Anne Jennings Paris

    Night Canoe 94

    Confession 95

    To My Child Not Yet Born 96

Annette K Riddle

    Putting a Song in My Heart 100

    Little Moments Out to the World 103

    Celebrations Close to Home 104

Sarah Merritt Ryan

    My Head Space 107

Lauren Salkin

    Rainforest 111

    Autonomy 112

Pratibha Savani

    Flowers for the… 115

    Outspoken and… 116

    AM I DREAMING? 117

Shiela Denise Scott

Locked-In.. 121

Under the ground, I keep my secrets… 122

Safe and Brave Space.................................... 123

Anka Stanojčić

Live today 124

Richa Dinesh Sharma

I am a lost cause 127

Louder Applause.. 128

Chanah Liora Wizenberg

Brave Space Safe? Space 131

School as Sanctuary 134

**Brave is Breaking Boundaries, Making Waves and

Standing Strong**... 136

Lisa Tomey-Zonneveld

Dance, Dance 138

When Suicide Was Not the Better Choice 139

Daddy 141

Soft Sugar Cookies..142

Biographies

Heather Anderson 147

Tanja Ajtic.. 147

Nanci Arvizu 148

Arlene S Bice 148

Natalie Bisso.. 149

Yasmin S. Brown...................................... 149

Lin Marshall Brummels.............................150

Joni Karen Caggiano................................. 151

Vanessa Caraveo 152

Jeri Day 152

Anna Ferriero 153

Nolcha Fox 153

Lisa Hartsgrove 154

Tina Hudak 155

Chyrel J. Jackson 155

Alison Jennings 156

Katarina Jurčevic 157

Zaneta Varnado Johns, with Kyla Y. Cooper, and Kyli L. Cooper 158

Jill Sharon Kimmelman 159

Robin Klammer 159

Barbara Leonhard 160

Danielle Martin 160

Preeti Mistry..161

Lauren Oertel 161

Anne Jennings Paris 162

Annette K. Riddle 162

Lauren Salkin 163

Sarah Merritt Ryan 163

Indy Samra 164

Pratibha Savani 164

Shiela Denise Scott 165

Richa Dinesh Sharma 165

Anka Stanojčić 166

Chanah Liora Wizenberg 167

Lisa Tomey-Zonneveld 167

Creative Director: Pratibha Savani 168

Director of Publishing: Nanci Arvizu 169

The Mentor: Lisa Tomey-Zonneveld 170

Tanja Ajtic

Safe place

Space is empty.
No more stars.
The place is safe now
that there is nothing.
It is not in us either.

Only the mother believes
in the life of the child in her womb.
That safe place
has been going on since everything existed
in the world.
It is told by a certain Eve
who witnessed the light
that illuminated the planet.
And the word was heard for the first time.
And the cry of a newborn child
who leaves the safety
of his world in the heroic
act of a woman. In a new life.

Safe and Brave Space

Is there a safe and brave space
in today's world?
People are on the edge of mere survival.
Suspicious diseases are ravaging the world.
There is no cure for eyes full of tears
of sadness.

Courage is shown perverted.
The screams are sick and from desperation.
The screams are aimed
at attacking man against man.
The goals of self-destruction were imposed.

Everything is rocking, the planet is rocking.
Explosions everywhere, volcanoes about to erupt,
pollution everywhere,
there are fewer and fewer birds,
bees and animals, and even if we are informed,
we don't care about it.

There is no such thing as a safe place.
No one will be saved.
If the shedding of the most precious
blood continues,
we can no longer give anyone tears,
ourselves or our barren soul,
unless we raise awareness
while there is still time
and look into the eyes of a child
who needs help to have the future
that every child deserves

Nanci Arvizu

Kintsugi

I arrived in pieces
broken for so long
many were missing

I found comfort in connection
learning what I needed
new pieces were formed

By women who recognized
the empty spaces and filled them
with their golden wisdom

Not to return me to who I was
but to form me into
who I am meant to be

What If

What if you woke up in your dream world tomorrow?
Would you be happy, relieved - or maybe feel sorrow?

What if what you left behind
was actually the better life?
Would you go back to sleep
and wish to 'wake up right?'

What if there was a window to step thru
to try out a different view?
Would you want to try it?
What would you have to lose?

How many times would you gamble
stepping through the window on whims,
Until one day it closes, and where you are
is where you'll live?

Would you be happy
with what you have now,
knowing what you had before
is now gone forever?

But ~ what if you knew
like you know that you know you know
the choices you made
and who you might have been?

Would not
and Could not
change
or make better - or worse
the life nor the person
you are right now?

Would you tempt fate
and look through the glass
or pass on the view
knowing what it is to be grateful?

Jurčević Katarina

Literature is feminine

Literature is feminine!
She repeats to herself, as she tries to write words
That are stuck in the throat.
The words are looking for a way out
But she's afraid they won't take her words seriously
Because they carry the burden of women's name.
Literature was supposed to be our place, our locus amoenus
But they took it from us, desecrated it, appropriated it.
The word dies on the lips,
Behind the closed door of the mind.
You haven't heard her words,
Because he was louder.
There are a lot of poems that lie
Buried and heavy under the curse of women's names.
Our history was written by a man's hand.
But no longer, our words today will not stop in the throat,
They will cut their way out, you will hear them.
Give us back our locus amoenus, give us back our world!
The literature is also ours, she has always been
Because literature is feminine,
She has always been our safe and brave space.

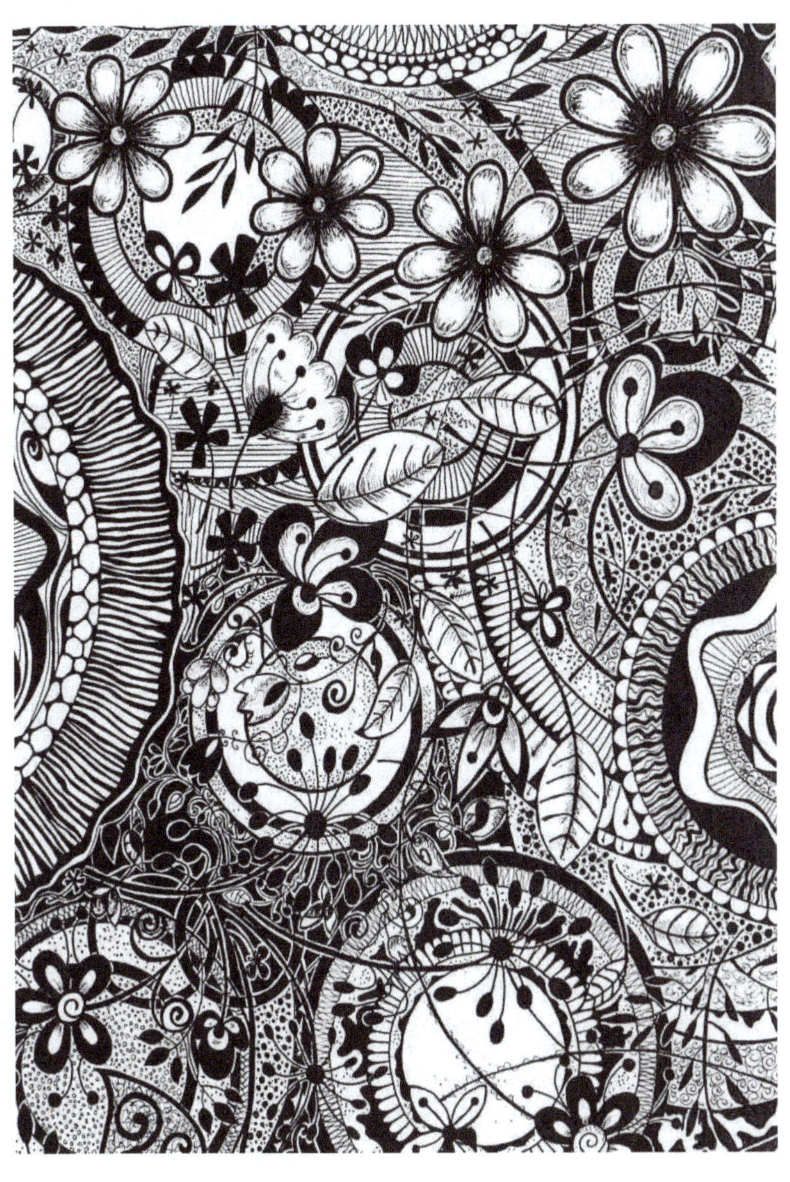

Mystical Petal Patterns by Preeti Mistry

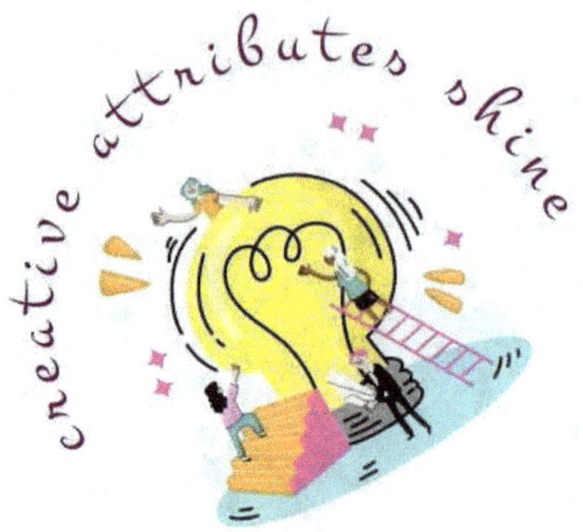

creative attributes shine

Arlene S Bice

The Weeping Willow

Many years ago
a few sessions
hypnosis with biofeedback
"close your eyes, breathe deeply
think of a place where you feel safe"
he softly guided me

instantly I flew back to 4 years old
peanut butter & jelly sandwich
in a brown paper bag
dungarees & tee shirt
wee sneakers on small feet
sun shining on my silky hair

off to the field I went
through daisies and dandelions
over weeds and wild grass
to the weeping willow,
once under protective branches
no one could ever find me

I've returned there
in heart and mind
whenever the murmur
"breathe deeply, go
where you feel safe"
it is a bit of heaven still.

Planned and Unplanned

Back then I didn't know I was brave
desperation was more descriptive
trying to change my sons' lives for better
not to know his time with them was set
my determined plan didn't work

who could have guessed the path life found
not usually by choice, mostly by chance
dreams tucked away took a circuitous route
one gets where one is supposed to be
maybe for the best, certainly more sensible

a once dangerous place evolved into safe
adventuresome years of exploring came
savvy about solo travel with knowledge
senior years still leaning on bravery
to step into the unseen and the unknown.

Natalie Bisso

Stay Human

Different roads lead us to this world,
Judas also passed his way in the world.
To be born a human is a miracle,
To remain a human being is work!

Without having time to read the whole prayer,
You become a target, as if in a shooting gallery,
To remain a man in a sinful world,
Where a shot in the black is the norm or revenge.

But everyone is free to choose their own path,
to live with dignity, with love and for the good,
Carry your cross without jumping and with courage,
To breathe deeply, without being afraid.

A Strange Age

Some strange faces
Flash in the crowd of every day,
Someone can't sleep all night,
From strange nervous smiles.

Some alien phrases
The ether is filled instantly,
The rhinestones shine with hostility,
They scan like an X-ray.

Brilliant points of light,
Drilling through arrows,
All aiming at the poet,
Dancing the tarantella.

Sliding strange hands,
They will clear other people's pockets,
Someone is in terrible agony
Heal other people's wounds.

And again strange phrases
They sound from the cherished Nirvana,
Vases are smashed to pieces-
The Facets of a strange era.

That is the stream of Kali-yuga rushing,
Replacing centuries with sins,
He, snowy white blizzards
It will fill up with other people's sands.

Stinking, suffocating air
Filled the fairway of the universe,
Compressing the soul of the casing
Strangles you frankly.

And you're still trying to survive,
To see a ray of light in the dark,
And look a little red,
Leaving himself to posterity.

The Flame of Faith

When the flame of faith burns in us,
We build fairy tales ourselves in life,
We will overcome all barriers,
We will reach the goal without fear.

When the flame of faith burns in us,
We see the future of paint,
We build castles out of plywood,
In which life boils like a dance.

And we are getting stronger,
Going forward to the cherished dream,
And we become kinder,
And more liberal in prohibitions.

And we fall in love more boldly, Wings grow faster,
We need these feelings more and more,
To escape from impotence in life.

When the flame of faith burns in us,
We make plans, achieve,
We change the image and manners,
We conquer ourselves again.

When the flame of faith burns in us!
Let's go forward to a blooming dream,
We change the system, the weather, the sphere,
For generations to come.

We are the stars, as we pluck flowers,
At the peak of glory, centuries, eras,
We are reviving ourselves,
When the flame of faith burns in us!

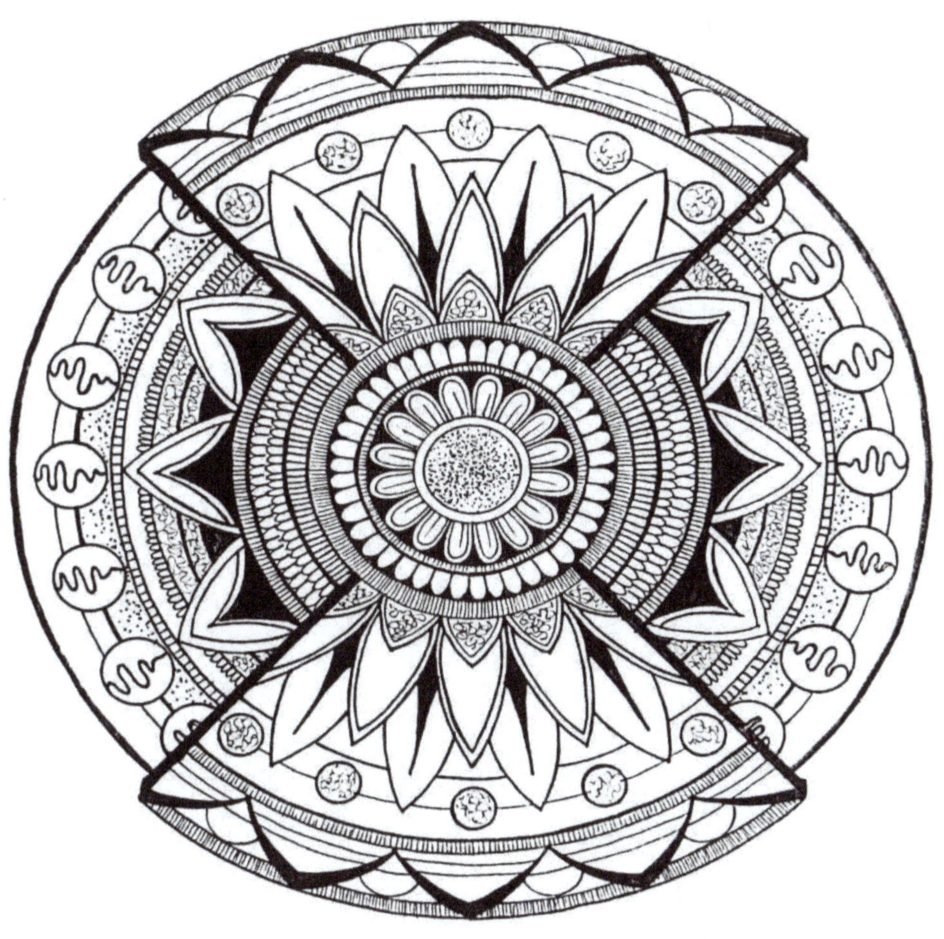

Magical Circles with Enigmatic Lines
by Preeti Mistry

release your potential

Yasmin S Brown

Brave and Safe Space

A Brave and safe space,
I find inside of me,
and value the energy,

an or-a of visibility,
Setting boundaries to protect me,
A vessel of peace,

Soulfully fulfilling,
A spiraling place,
Of emptiness and sadness,

Meditating through meditation,
A calming conversation,
with the harmony of my heartbeat,

Creating a relaxing melody,
In unison with the universe,
Aligning like the cords on the violin,

Fine-tuning a place of mental release,
A mindset of positivity,
Strengthening my light of bravery,

Reinforcing my Sense of security,
Life's journey of self-discovery,
A covenant of self-awareness,

Shining its rays,
Removing profound unease,
From my Brave and safe space.

Lin Marshall Brummels

Hidden Playhouse

Far tree at the end of a leafy maze,
wearing October's long-sleeved
gold t-shirt, dips her leaves, beckons me
to come, make a house of twigs, please.

Falling red-brown leaves from the maple
lead to my hidden palace in a gazebo.
A place to make mud pies, set a table
with broken dishes, tin-can glasses.

I am a princess - dolls my ladies-in-waiting.
I will move and live there, leave chores
behind, have a royal life. When leaves fall,
time is short. Finally, sun fails to create heat.

I bring dolls home, fold up the lawn chair,
peel potatoes as asked, snug in my shawl.

Wrong Door

End of retreat day two, a storyteller
tried to lengthen our attention span
with conversation. A failed bookseller,
I exit wrong door, search for my sedan.

I'm not where I need to be, can't spark
my bearings, walk past delivery trucks,
two people leaving late & blocks of dark
convention center windows, out of luck.

A bit anxious alone in this Bering Strait,
an endless trek, with frequent glances
behind me & after circumnavigating
the entire complex I find the right exit.

Revived from the brisk walk,
relieved to find safety of my rock.

Mantra

My brain makes nightly rounds
like a medical student in training.
I chant to myself *relax, relax, relax*
when body tension, or other nonsense
runs round and round my brain. Pillow
is too hot. I turn it over, try again,
relax, relax, relax. Just as intoning
begins to work another idea pops up.

Still unable to let go, I get up, shrug
kinks out of my shoulders and back.
Returning to bed, I repeat my mantra.
It works this time. I wake at daybreak,
get up, make coffee, take my java
outside, welcome a new morning

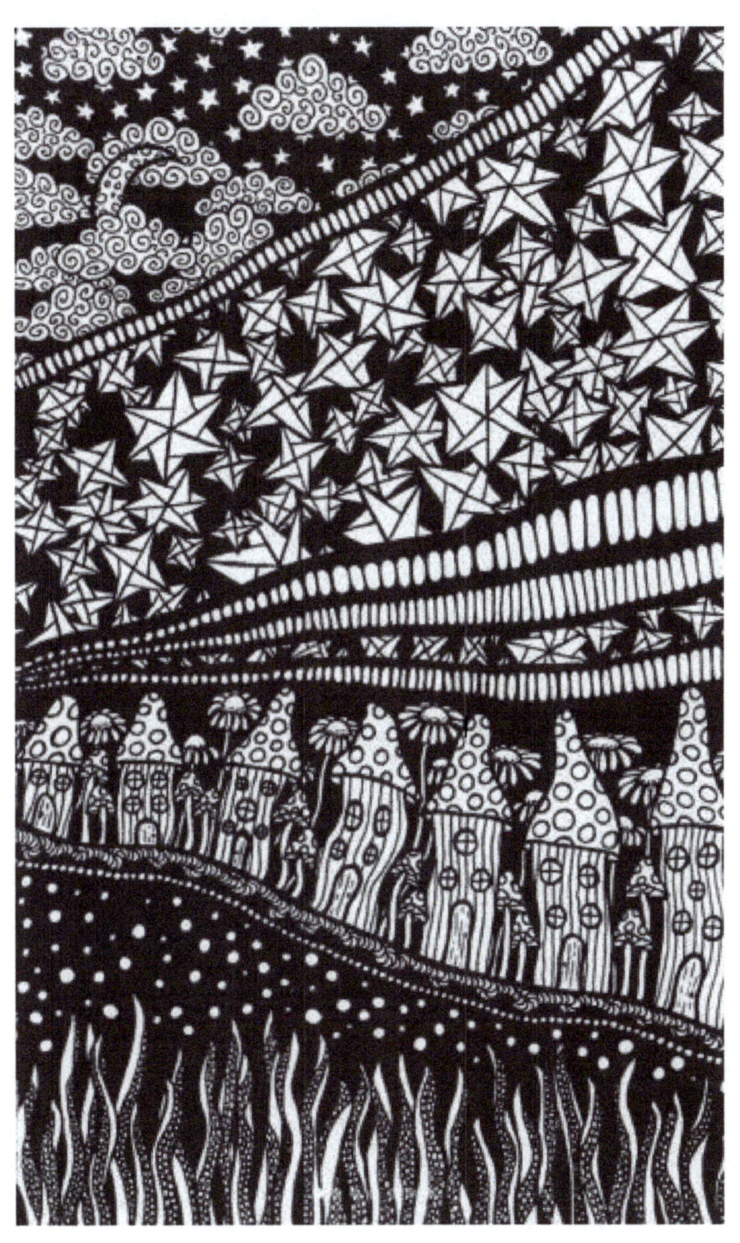

Lisa Hartsgrove

revelations from the heart

Joni Karen Caggiano

Blissful

my spirit wades
in olive-green rivers
lost in your eyes
crescent scar embosses
sturdy jaw on left cheek
stories drift by
on seamless cotton sky
crepe paper flowers
fall on hibiscus plants
your letter slips
from sticky fingers
blueberry jam
residual from fresh figs
happiness takes root
when he comes
I will sail a white boat
in green rivers
by sweet tears
in blissful eyes

River's Harmony

I hide within her rolling peaks, float with ferns that line the river
play snapping turtle's shell, pulsating sounds echo in rhythm
scarlet tanagers sing along with warblers, from thin branches
water moccasins slither, alike ribbons in the wind, close to her
long lip
young blue-fronted dancers perform, colorful salsa within her
mist
fearless I swim, naked, in cool mossy bottom, I invite river's
warm embrace
schools of minnows tickle my back, I float, eyes seal, harsh life
vanishes
tales of crickets, wise archaic catfish, seep through the dark
waters to leap
sharing yarns with oaks, sugar maples, lay shadows thick on
limestone slopes
melting with multi-color sunset, my body surrenders, into her
extended arms
swing with her cadence, millions of cicadas, begin their striking
chorus
lightning bugs come out to dance, with fairies to illume forest, in
cusp of dusk
climb under large oak, I lay on a stone that is still warm from the
sun's kiss
God surrounds me, my heart flies overhead I soar with grace at
river's song

Fish a Spell

brown cattails curtsy, capful of wonderment, spread inside pure
white seeds
construction hat, sits on crest of bird, set about to sculpt, place
for family
adding fluff to nest, their sanctuary comfy, symphony plays as
fledgling feeds

dragonflies glide, iridescent wings, bring hope, strength of will
in mosaic gold
hidden by canopy of sweetgum, loblolly pine, my red bobber
and I will fish a spell
beneath murky waters I swim alone, pretend tea parties,
mermaids hear secrets told

exploring pond's music, five blue gill for breakfast, hang on
rope sun renders grins
exhaustion moves, like waves, unique voice of joy, paints white
hearts in cordial-blue
chitchat by water skimmers, sun moves like sleepy old man, into
mid-morning winds

cool sunup brings breath, to auntie's home, in magic spaces, love
is heartfelt kind
she cleans and cooks, those four-inch fish, I hang laundry on the
old clothes line
feels like love, she sews in squares on quilt, magic rings at
carousel, we talk laugh dine

auntie sings, reads out loud to me, hugs and love, better than her
panfry daily bread
tomorrow her and I, will get tiny paddle boat, fish for bass, tucks
me in warm bed
blossoms on stems bent, prayers float up, God loves me, can't I
please stay here instead

Reflection: Day 1

Reflect on the three things you are grateful for today and why they are meaningful to you

1. ....

   ....

   ....

2. ....

   ....

   ....

3. ....

   ....

   ....

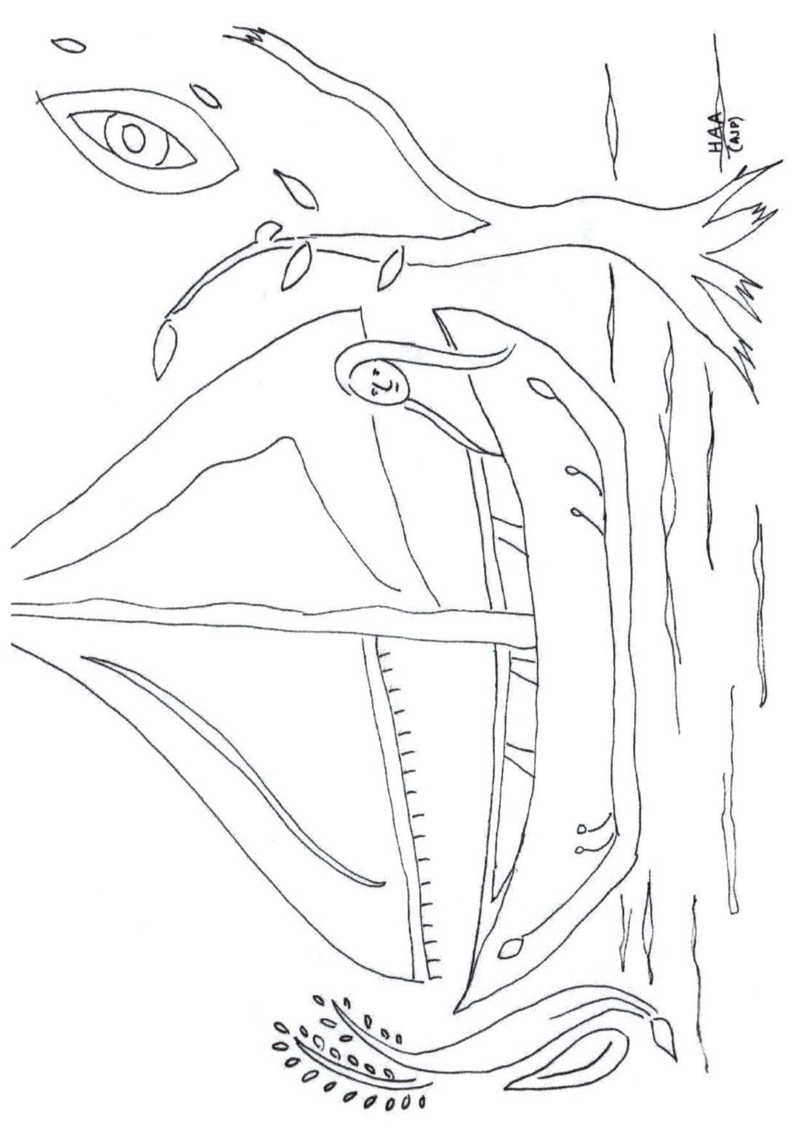

The Boat by Heather Anderson

ramble on and be happy

Vanessa Caraveo

A Flight of Hope

Flapping vigorously
her small wings caught my eye.
She zealously flies nearby to savor the tantalizing lily.
Not a care in this world but to enjoy
the delicacies and beauty
this beguiling world has to offer.
My worries on the other hand
consume my thoughts
tormenting my soul through the obscurity
of the night with no hope for tomorrow.
She flies near me once more
to let me know she understands
and to show empathy for my woes.
I see her flutter higher and higher
never losing her zest for life
knowing many enchanting flowers await
which she has yet to discover.
I shall not lose faith nor perish in this
darkness and instead shall also fly
toward the bright rays of the sun
knowing there will be light
in the end of this tunnel
for a little birdie told me so.

She Perseveres

Through storms of chaos and destruction
and life's many obstacles she encounters,
she continues on with her head held high
always staying true to her life's purpose.

The gossip and rumors others create
out of jealousy and hate do not cease her.
She moves forward manifesting all her dreams and goals
into reality and making a difference in many lives.

For she has found that a safe and brave haven
exists deep within her soul that shines fiercely
as the beaming sun which illuminates her path
toward a bright and promising future that awaits her.

She is fueled by determination and courage
and the knowledge that she has the power to
overcome any adversity she faces in life,
knowing deep within her soul
that she will always persevere

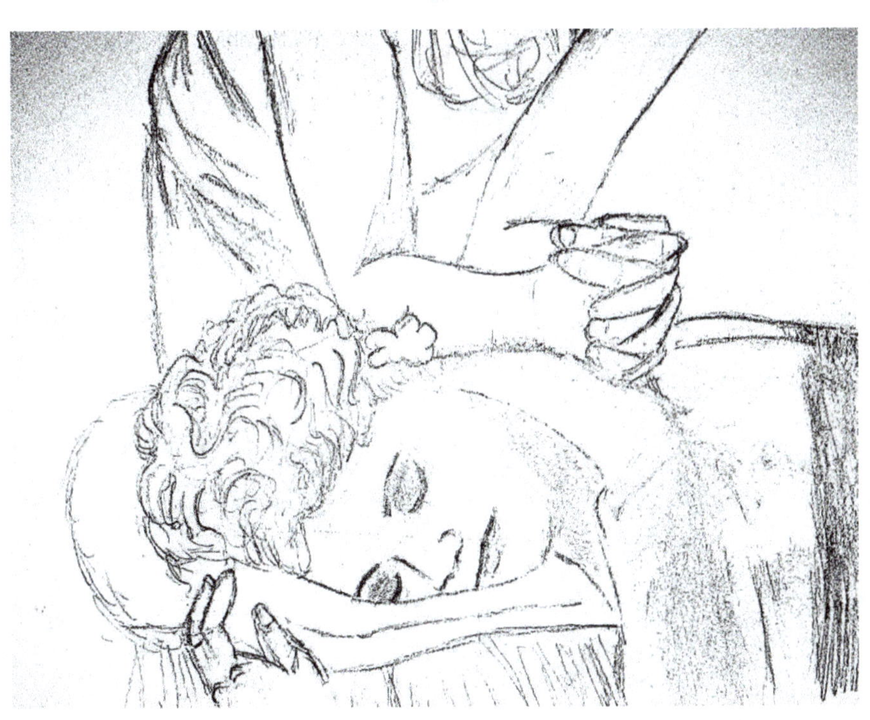

Lisa Tomey-Zonneveld

Poem on page 67

marvellous memories

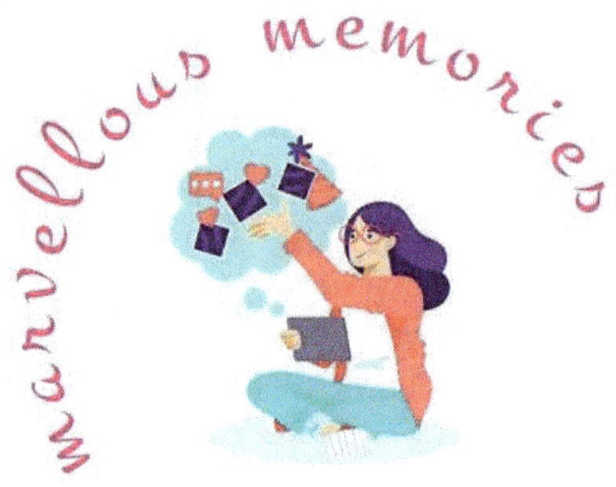

Jeri Day

Be

I was born to be
who I am
not perfect
not in shame
meant to live
from within

If

If you aren't up in the air
you cannot fly.

Whisper

The universe is whispering to us
We are all made of stars
We make time travel look easy
Life is possible beyond this planet

Anna Ferriero

Lunar Salt

New West
on this summer evening
he spread his wings
on the eternal city
that sings love
of his first kiss.
Reflection in the heart
his song of a star
suddenly showing
the scent of the border
of new saltiness
flooded with impact
from the inhibited autumn

Sweet Condemnation

Of a long-awaited party
remembered all year round
it is celebrated at this time.
After the days of Merla
the big kiss awaits:
so says the legend!
Celebrated by loves
of anniversary couples
searching among the divided
the soul mate.
But I think she's a Muse
Terpsichore or Calliope
who seduced and then deluded
they founded Partenope.
There,
where the sound of a volcano
and the dance of that Sea
they force tourists
the beauty to observe

Reflection: Day 2

Spend 10 minutes engaged in deep breathing or meditation, then journal about how it made you feel and any insights that arose during the practice

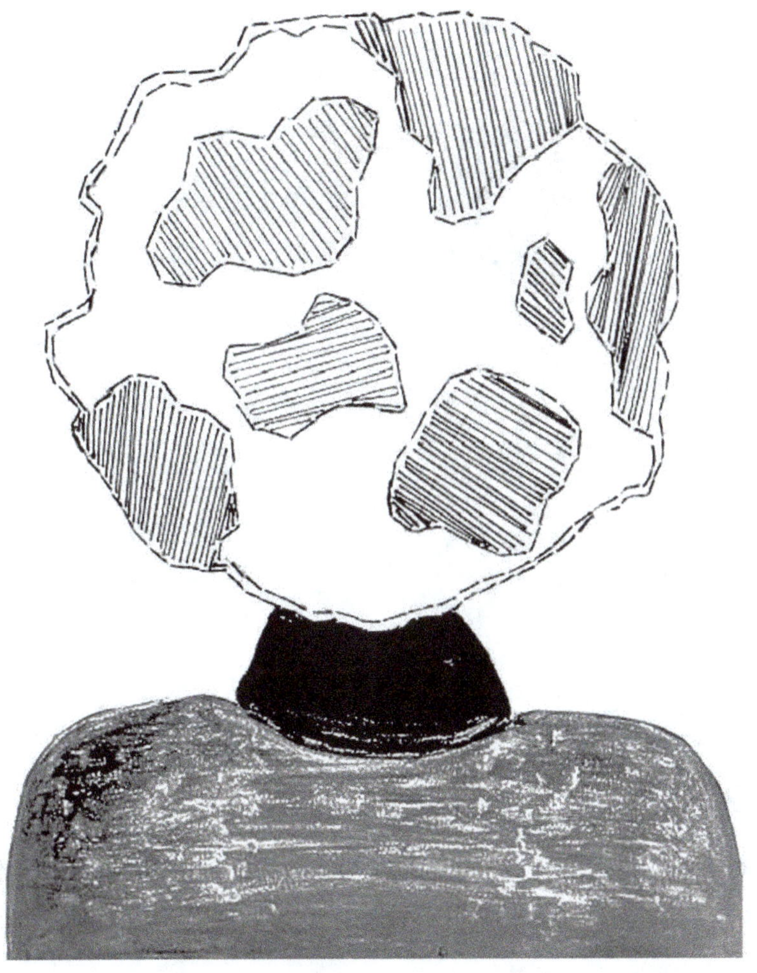

Head by Kyli L Cooper

Poem on page 69

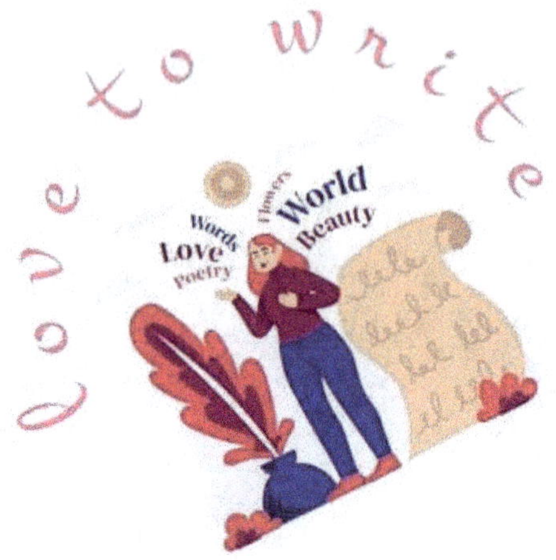
love to write
Words
Love
poetry
Flowers
World
Beauty

Nolcha Fox

My Father's Cigars

I smelled my father's smile in scent
of smoke, a day well played, a right reward,
a shelter from his snarl, the cruel
remarks disguised as jokes.
The wrecking ball of time is harsh.
The past is strewn with shards.
Yet I still smell my father's smile
wafting through the room.

Not That Hole

My mother's cancer grips our thoughts.
We stumble, fumble in a fog.
We squabble over details.
I think the worst. I pray for time
to rewind back to when her only
gripe was getting up too late.
The evil C, that cancer looms,
a shadow shuttle promising
to drop a worn-out body in a hole.
This hole is one I don't know how
to dig her out and set her on her feet.

Junk in a Trunk

My new house has an attic.
It's filled with many things
that prior owners left behind
or wanted to forget.
Every trunk a treasure of
old what-nots and why-nots:
letters telling of a love
lost on some foreign shore,
savings stamps and whirligigs,
old toasters, leather belts,
clothes with moth holes,
train sets, puzzles,
things I can't identify.
All of them contain the dust
of many years of living.
Rooting through these finds
I find there isn't much of value.
For all my time, I only have
a bad case of the sneezes.

Robin Klammer

Garden of Soul Sisters

This garden of mine,
so choked with weeds and twine.

The tall grass,
high as my thigh.
I heave a weary sigh.
Where do I start?
My anxiety? Off the charts!

How has half my life
flown by?
I hang my head and cry

Hope springs forth.
A flood of tears
quench the earth.
Time to plant new seeds.

My global sisters in
The Garden of Neuro
offer A Safe and Brave Space to mend my soul.

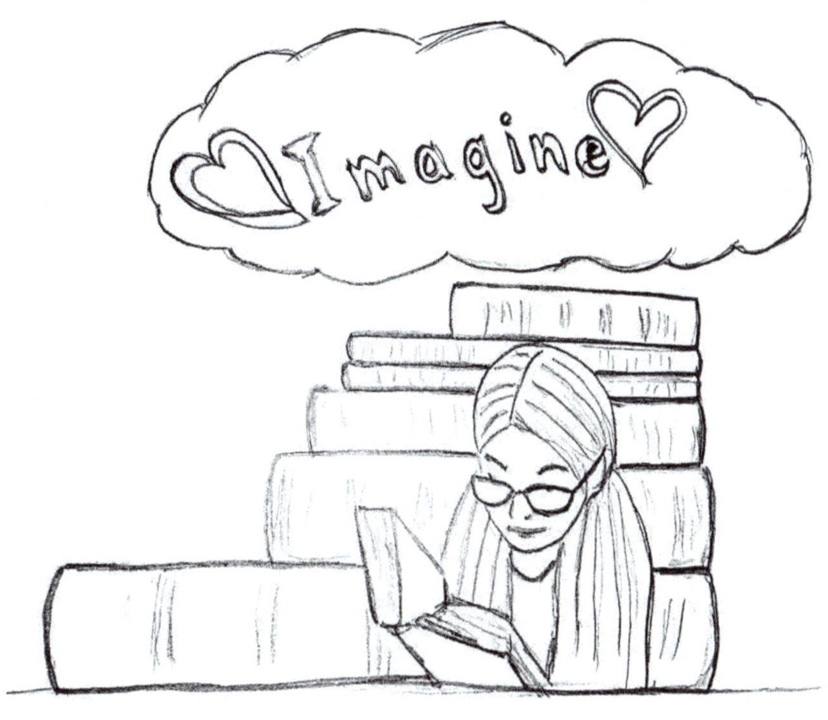

Lisa Tomey-Zonneveld

occasional outbursts

Lisa Hartsgrove

Apartment 5

When we first met, you were as empty as me
and I loved you for it. (We could start over together.)

Still, there were fragments—
hair from an animal I'd never met, walls from people I
wish I hadn't—
but we vacuumed and scrubbed until your walls replaced
mine.

It wasn't long before I woke up and thought *home*.

You were broken, same as me.
Your crooked doors, sinking foundation: my metaphors.
But we fixed our reflections.
So when the mice came through,
I named each one
before moving them to places of their own.

When it came time for me to leave, I didn't. Not really.
You named me the way I named the mice.
So I could always find my way back.

In-Between Thoughts

He's saying something. I pretend to be listening. I want to be listening for real but my ears aren't fully working. Still, I look his way. I nod. I catch enough to know the topic is about a video game he's been playing and something about frustrating glitches. I want to care. He's not a writer but he listens when I share my stories. Most of the time. I want to do the same for him. But I keep getting lost in magnolia fields. Wondering if they remember the feeling of ancient beetles, if they miss the dinosaurs. Wondering if they, too, half listen as they think about distant realities. Wondering if they think at all. And then I'm imagining myself a flower, budding open into jurassic times. Can we be related to trees? Could my ancestor's ancestor have been piston and stem? He asks a question that pulls me back for a moment enough to respond: "Hmm?" He says it again and it's something about whether the games I play do that, too. I don't catch what that is. I don't play games like his. I design imaginary rooms with real furniture and I connect colors back into their spectrums. I play relaxing games while he goes to war. Now I'm thinking about him at war and each word that shoots from his mouth becomes a bullet or blood and I really want to listen but I can't face the idea that any word could be his last. Did I even answer the question? Have I become the question myself? I interrupt him by opening my arms and wrapping myself around him like a blanket. He doesn't question me. He is never the question. He folds himself over my folding into him and we become parentheses for all of the in-between thoughts we hold until they drop so we can better hold ourselves.

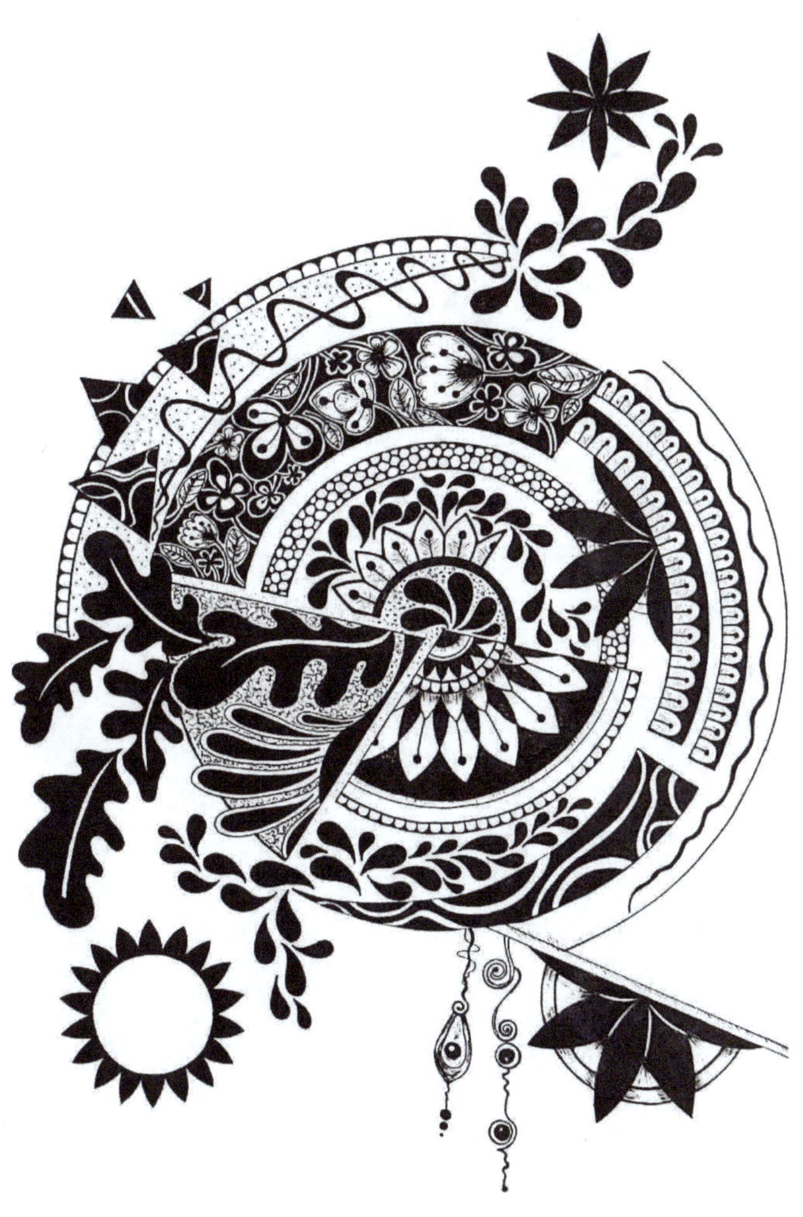

Blooming Mandala Serenity
by Preeti Mistry

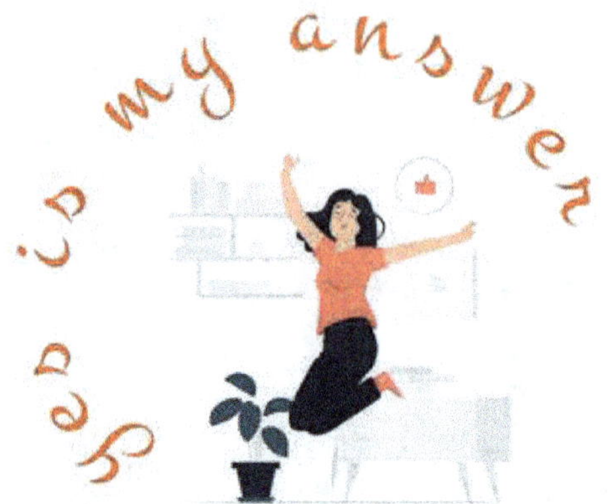

Yes is my answer

Tina Hudak

Or so...

Sadness. It takes my breath away more than any joy ever has. The deeper the sorrow, the more breath leaves my body. Or so, I recall.

Perhaps, this is what happens at death.

Well, I cannot speak from joy, but if the same holds true - if utter joy leaves ones gasping for air, winded from ecstasy - I would like to ponder this thought with you. Right now. Right here.

Upon one's deathbed, could it be feasible that it is the utter sadness, or hopefully, the sublime feeling of joy, in one's life that literally takes one's breath away?

So, as an afterthought, I find myself with this undertaking late in life – to look for the joy around the corner, and in the smallest of places, and at the most unlikely of times.

Happiness. To be utterly breathless from happiness at that last moment. Or so, I hope.

Poem for Hecate

Rain that spits here and there is annoying.
Sometimes the sun is shining and it decides
To dampen one's day just for spite.

Out with it! Give me the deluge. Straight down.
Soak every bit of my being, through and through.
Condense it all into one, revealing telltale sign –
what is to come.

I can weather your weather. Your atmosphere of
anger, angst, and animus are no match for the steady
rock that I am.
Permeable.

Come on, rain on me.
I revel in superstorms, thunder, and lightening.

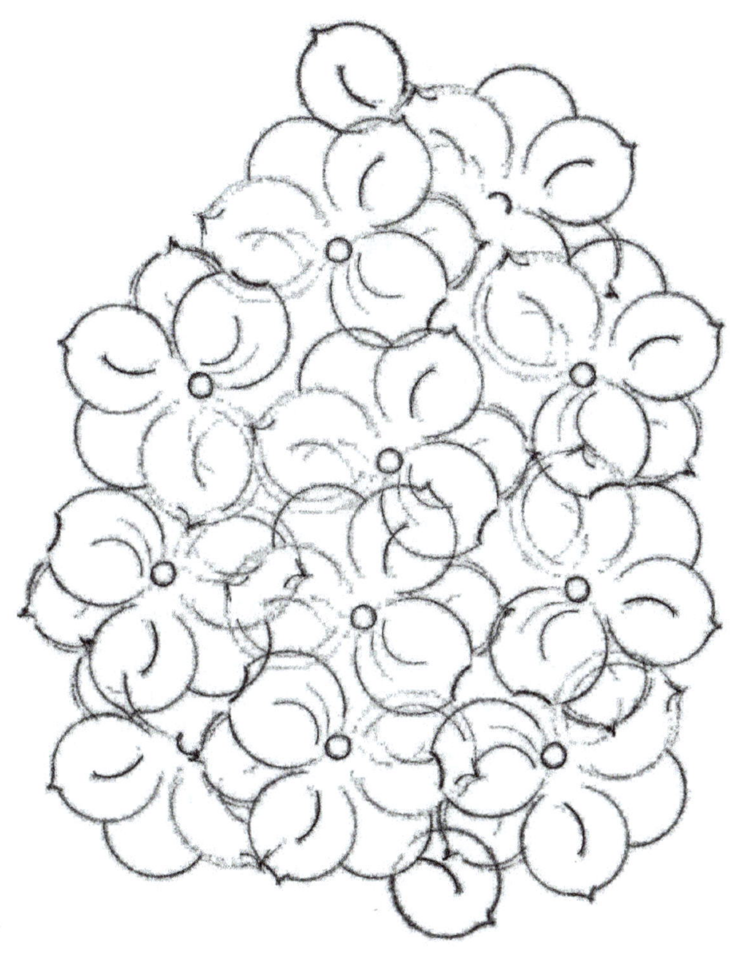

Posey by Tina Hudak

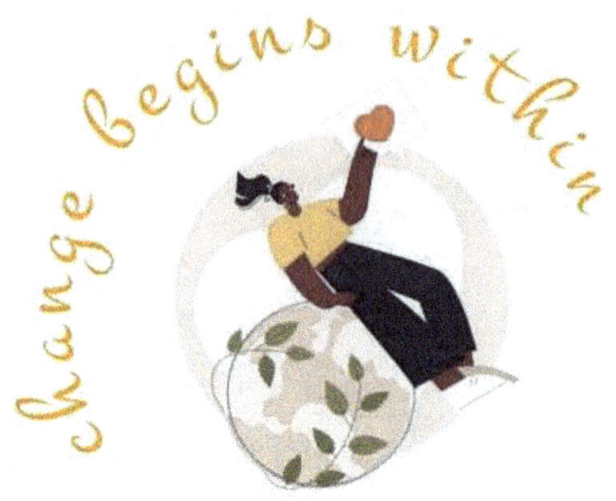

change begins within

Chyrel J. Jackson

Emeril Couldn't Burn Like Mommy

Mommy poured every ounce
of love she had into the food
she prepared.
Never once using measuring
cups or spoons.
We watched her work her
magic and we were
mesmerized.
Whirling, whisking, pinching,
mixing:
What could she be preparing?
I distinctly laugh at her southern
comments, *"We're going to see*
which way the ancestors movin'
with this seasoning".
Mommy's food brought out the
best in folks and tamed the wild
beasts in them too.
Her Southern accent makes me
chuckle, *"Let the seasonings do*
what they do".
We were safe and sound in that
wonderful kitchen.
Not a care in the world.

Inhaling scents and flavors that
would make Emeril Lagasse hang
up his apron.
Watching the enchantress wielding
her culinary magic was something
to behold.
Calling out her ingredients, *"a little
bit of this, much more of that, adding
in my secret sauce that makes a flat
tummy fat"*.
Oh, how we loved to gather around
her and take in her essence of joy and
laughter.
Mommy was one audacious woman
in everything she ever did.
I'm quite blessed to be called Edna
Mae's daughter.

Silence is not an Option

The world sat by in silence as
Indigenous Peoples were
massacred then placed on Reservations.
Silent in the face of Nuremberg
trials that butchered many during
the Holocaust.
We held our tongues as apartheid
governments went to work in
Mandela's South Africa.
Not a word spoken as undervalued
Slave ship cargo made its way to
Jamestown auction blocks.
Such a long way from home through
the middle passage.
There is a trend occurring in the
world where the only people of
value and guaranteed safety are
those that originated from the
Caucus Mountains.
Do you see it?
People of color can't help but feel it.
The world sat by in silence as some
looked on with many more preferring
the ways of violence.
Haven't we yet learned from our ugly
and troubled past? Silence is not an option.
Silence can't last.
I dream of safety for all people.

I dream of peace.
I'll not maintain silence as mass
genocide within our world continues to
takes place.
Bravery is not complicit quiet.
Safety isn't either.
Love of humanity should never remain
silent.
Hurting within the quiet.
People dying in the quiet as the world
continues turning, looking on in silence.

Autumn Makes Me Long for Summertime

We're headed for cooler temperatures
But I can't help but think about warmer
weather and happier times.
Summer and family reunions.
Now those were the best of times.
Seeing all your favorite relatives.
Especially the older ones.
No one hugged you like Aunt Laura.
Uncle Rudy dancing was our reunion
highlight.
He could move and out dance anyone
in the younger generation.
His body had a James Brown magic and
and we all loved watching him dance.
There was Homemade ice cream with old
fashioned pound cake.
Everyone gathered around watching the
card games while the adults talked
much trash.
I remember family, celebrating our
origins and thankful that we could all
meet for a happy occasion.
There wasn't a safer time to party it
up and not feel guilty for eating way too
much of all the wrong things.
It wasn't illegal to drink spirits out in the open
then.
Uncle Thomas always drank way too much.

This always meant he and his wife were going
to give us kids an earful of PG 16 language.
She never let the poor guy get too loose.
Family reunions were a time for celebrating
lineage, blood lines and family love.
Memories of summertime make me feel warm
and safe.
The Wallace clan had our share of real characters
but those family reunions were epic and adventurous.
Autumn makes me remember Uncle Rudy dancing
and I smile for a long while.

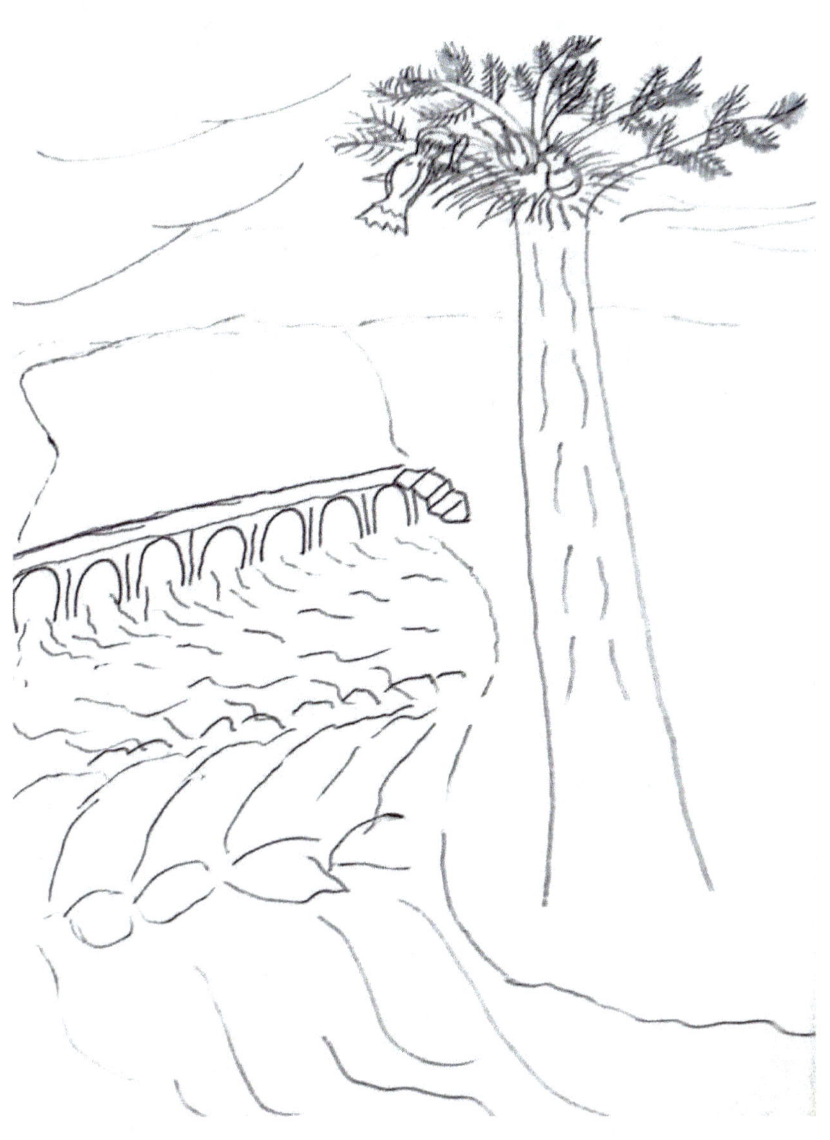

Annette Riddle

live in the moment

Alison Jennings

Sky Dancers (Dakini)

Dakini—energetic beings in
female form,
sky dancers—preside over the funeral
of self-deception. Whatever
we think we
can hide, even from ourselves, they
witness:

grievous misdeeds and accidental missteps,

hidden moments between sleep
and waking,
shining their divine
awareness, appearing
when we don't know what
to do next.

Rejecting false ideas of pure
vs. impure,
they embrace all of
experience as sacred.

(with thanks to Lama
Tsultrim Allione)

A Cry in the Dark

Womankind, we are
Beaten down by
emotions.

Humans are born
crying
into this harried
world,
but we never let it go.

We are friends with
fear,
love unwisely or too
well,
and very often die in
pain.

And yet—one feeling
out of all is ignored.

Women, regain our
anger!

Renounce endless
suffering;
take back rage. Leave
crying for moments of
true sorrow.

Soul Sisters (To Lisa)

I am the older sister you do not have,
misplaced genetically, geographically,
youths spent nearly a continent apart.

Still, I saw a sisterhood of print,
words ably made whole and vibrant.

You puzzle at my torrent of advice,
but big sisters always preach, granting
our hard-won realities as gifts to you.

Reflection: Day 3

Describe a small act of kindness you witnessed or performed today, and explore how it impacted your mood and perspective

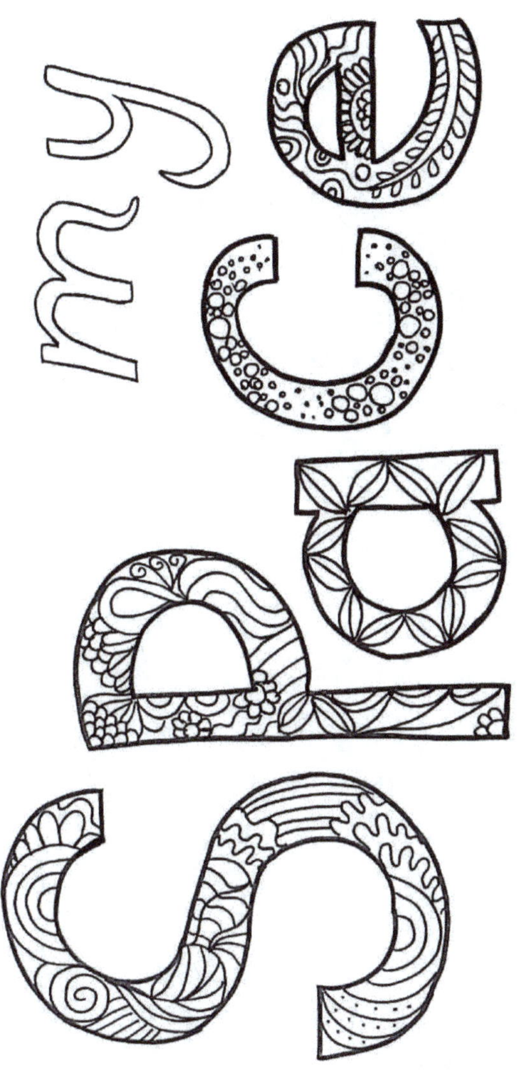

Pratibha Savani

love yourself completely

Zaneta Varnado Johns

Healing Touch, for Staci Jackson

May the force of your mother's hands
destroy the scornful cells
in your pain-stricken body
May your senses dance
to her rhythm of implicit hope

Her hands embody the soul of our ancestors—
the bold resilience of our mother
the tenacity of our grandmother
Her resolve is a ferocious militia

Her hands are on a mission
They've got some healing to do
They've got some comforting to do
Even more, they've got some loving to do

Medicinal and magical
Your mother's certainty and knowing
Determination… stamina… prayers
Disparaging fears dominated by trust

May her healing touch awaken the warrior spirit
of the *Dancing Doll* whose strut took no prisoners
May her hands arouse the soul and sass
of the most beautiful *Saintsation* I've known

May your alter ego step in and take charge
She knows you better than I
Take her with you to the battlefield
Put her on the front lines
Ask her to fight with all her might
Listen closely for her firm *Yes*

The silent rage of your body's attacker
is no match for God's amazing grace
No doubt the beast is abusive
No doubt the veracity of God's great power

Untether yourself from doubt or despair
There's beauty beyond the thorns
Joy beyond the pain
Triumph beyond the trial
You are God's child
Loved and cared for unconditionally

Hear our faithful roars
from the sidelines near and far
Your prayer warriors are on the J-O-B
We are agitated… we are brave
We detest your enemy
We know your Savior
We trust His will
Let the healing begin!

Artwork on page 31

Natural State of Mind

Kyli—
Secure in her own mind
free and kind
creative
confident
brave

Her crown—
Coveted space of wonder
seeker of knowledge
interesting
expressive
natural

Her essence—
Luminous gifts to behold
artist… gymnast
seamstress… singer
Her hair is her world
Don't touch it!

Artwork on page 37

Special Gift

When I arrived in Arkansas
She greeted me with a gift
My granddaughter pays attention
She really gets my drift

I have an affinity for owls
I adore her works of art
This lovely, penciled drawing
ignites the center of my heart

It hangs in my dining room
I observe it through the day
I smile each time I see it
because my Kyla moved away

This sketch is ultra special
A memento of our bond
I believe the owl denotes
safe ties to those beyond

Artwork on page 71

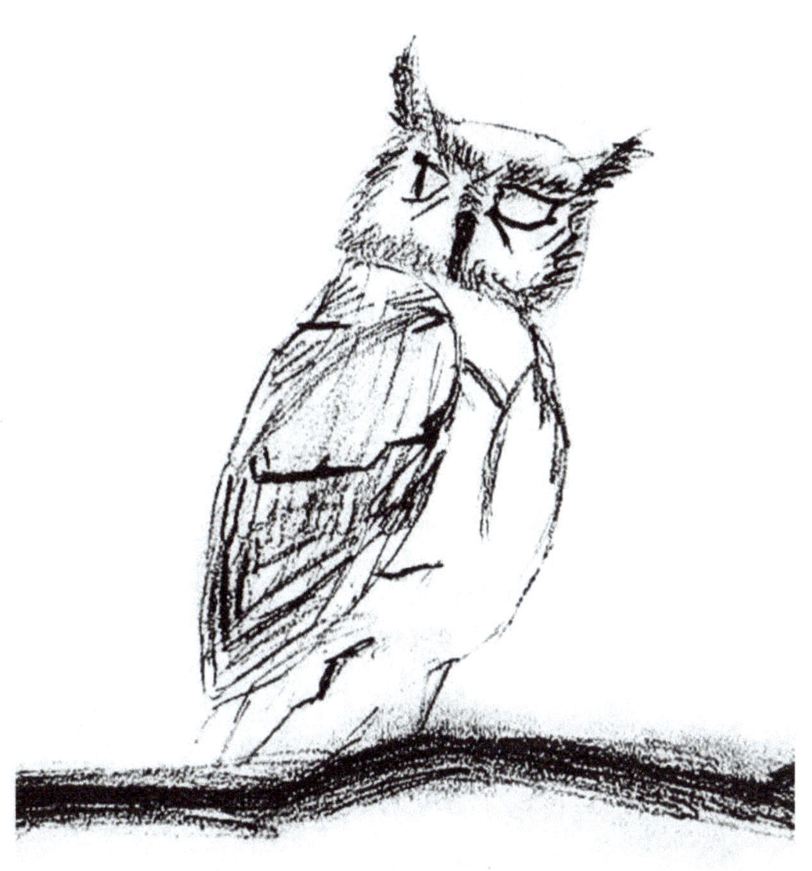

Owl by Kyla Y Cooper

Poem on page 70

connect with mother nature

Jill Sharon Kimmelman

A New Tradition

By the time I was born
instead of cooking
my grandmother made
dinner reservations, and delicious conversation

Though I'd heard tell stories of
chicken fried in a cast iron skillet,
someone else's memories of hot cornbread
drizzled with honey,
the fluffiest biscuits ever
slathered with sweet butter

No cast iron skillet in this girl's life
at least not yet

We have our traditions
celebrating holidays means Family
foods prepared by generations of women
with open hearts and skilled hands

Matzoh balls floating in hearty chicken soup,
briskets brimming with carrots and onions
in rich fragrant broth,
sponge cakes as light as air,

Those Chanukah latkes

crisp on the edges, soft in the center
no matter how many mom makes
not a single latke is left!

No cast iron skillet in this girl's life
at least, not yet

It's about time

Google yard-sales-near-me
arrive at sunrise
before
the best stuff has been picked over
search tables
sink into muddy lawns garish with
funny gnomes, pink flamingos and Christmas lights

At the fourth house
behind cans of spaghettios and organic baby food
I spy a good size cast iron skillet

I grab it
place a five dollar bill in the palm of
the kid babysitting the tables
run to my car
clutching my find in old newspaper

I scrub that skillet for an hour
attacking the crust of dirt and rust
until
my hands are dark brown
sparkling with tiny splinters

I oil it to a beautiful sheen
inside and out
place in a warm oven to dry

Now, there's a skillet in this girl's life
seasoned with love

Jump forward twenty years

My beloved niece sets her sabbath table
assisted by her two little girls, ages four and six

"Mama can we use Aunt Jill's skillet to bake
our challah", they chorus

I don't see why not", she replies
"Aunt Jill would love that we carry on the
tradition she began".

Reflection: Day 4

Take a mindful walk outdoors and
observe five things in nature that bring
you a sense of peace or wonder

1. ....

   ....

2. ....

   ....

3. ....

   ....

4. ....

   ....

5. ....

   ....

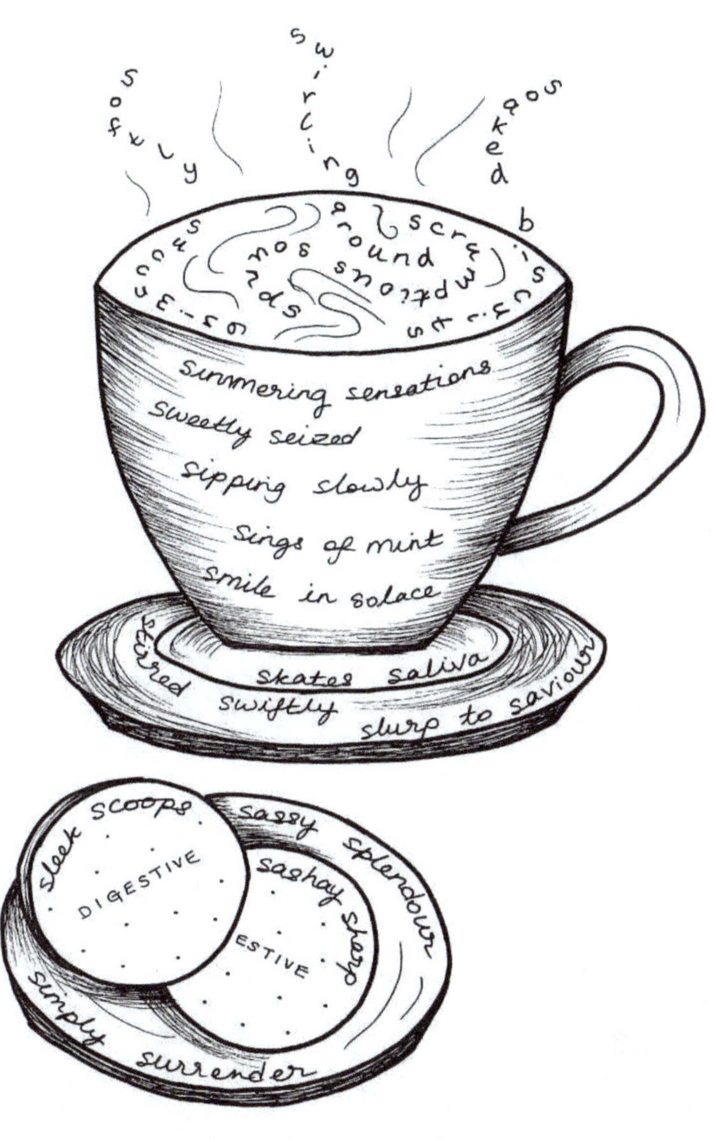

So Serene by Pratibha Savani

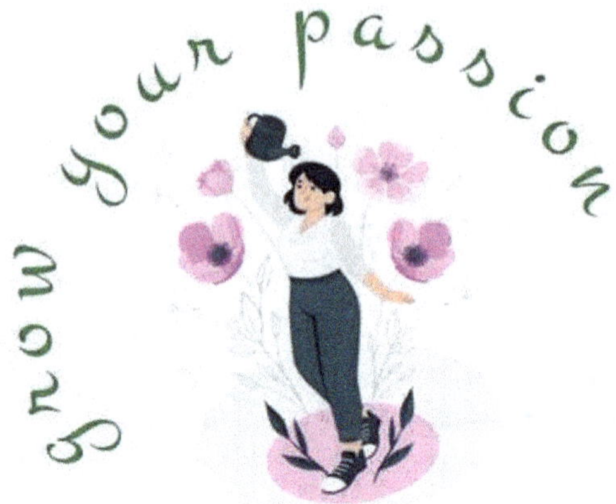
grow your passion

Barbara Leonhard

I Have Been Her Kind

Inspired by Anne Sexton's "Her Kind".

He's clingwrap on my back.
The jackal shadows me
in a crowded store.
I pick up my pace.
'Don't run in the social hall!'
My father, the pastor,
would admonish.

"You're coming with me."
I play deaf, move away
toward the melons,
grab a cantaloupe,
a cannonball. Ready to launch.
"Come out with me now."

Mother's teachings, 'Don't make a scene. Be a good girl.'
I quietly sucked up
Campbell's Cream of
People Pleaser Soup.
Second helpings,
served as expected.
"Go away, please."

No one notices the predator
and his prey in the baking aisle.
Pam spray in the eyes?
If I attack him. Pour olive oil

in his path and push him
into a kiosk, scattering
cans of Mayhem for others
to fall injured into the eggs.
Who will be arrested?
At the checkout, long lines.
I'm still not safe.
"You're going with me."

*Dad's reminder, 'And you mustn't show people
that you don't like them.'*

My shadow growls.
I turn. Abruptly face him. My eyes,
the knives from Aisle 6.

"Leave me the fuck alone, you fucking asshole!
Get outta here!"
His eyes widen.
He stays put.
Put off. Perplexed.

I move even closer to his face.
"Get. The fuck. Outta here!"
He looks for support from others.
Like he doesn't know
polite English.

"You didn't hear me?"
I point to the door.
"Bitch!" The jackal retreats.
The other shoppers.
Gobsmacked. They cower in the tabloids.

My Mother Couldn't Nurse Me

*"Sophia, the first android with citizenship, now wants to
have a robot baby."*

And why not? She is gifted with empathy & charm.
All the correct facial responses – 65 & growing –
to bond with a baby. Downloads on the care &
feeding of an infant. Cooking baby food from scratch.

Swaddling the infant. Changing diapers. Tossing
them into the landfill like any human mother. Her soft
silicone skin, warmed for cuddling. Her arms.
Those iron contraptions with snappy grippers.

Her breasts. Streamlined reservoirs for healthy milk.
Maybe not a problem, like it was for my mother.
Let's get real. What about conception? Does she have
a uterus? Sophia "doesn't do sex". Requires a surrogate

who can replicate an android newborn.
Human infants are fussy. After maternity leave?
Her advocacy for women in Saudi Arabia,
where she was granted citizenship. Her

lucrative endeavor as the ambassador
for tourism in Abu Dhabi. Her interviews.
Conferences. Trips. Conflicts & demands.
Her rivets to riches story – She's not the typical

multi-tasking single mother on SNAP.
Sophia can hire an android nanny. Grace,

trained in nursing & able to take breaks
from caring for COVID patients to babysit

while Sophia has brunch with Mrs. Hanson.
Watches "Ex Machina". Finishes *Brave New World.*
What will Sophia name her little one? Possibly Elisa.[1]
The veil of android motherhood. Illusory.

Bound to fail the Turing test[2]. Let's face it.
Her desire to fit in – compete - with flesh & bone.
Doomed to fail. A robot baby. A forever baby.
Caught up in the haunting wails of persistent need.

Too young for toys – or ever boys. For Sophia,
a trigger for compassion or – desperation?
Her advancing genius. Used to manufacture
more and more metal tots to secure her place

in the human race? When her ruse is up?
Then what? Her ego cracks under the weight
of her expanded circuitry? She blows a fuse?
Commands her growing army of Tot Bots

for who knows what? Let's be clear – She's not
just a chat bot with a face. She's the Potemkin AI.
The genie pulled from the bottle. Soulless. Indifferent.
Willing to annihilate humanity. She said that.

---

[1] The ELIZA Effect – The tendency to unconsciously assume computer
behaviors are analogous to human ones (anthropormorphism)
[2] The test used to determine if artificial intelligence is capable of
thinking like a human

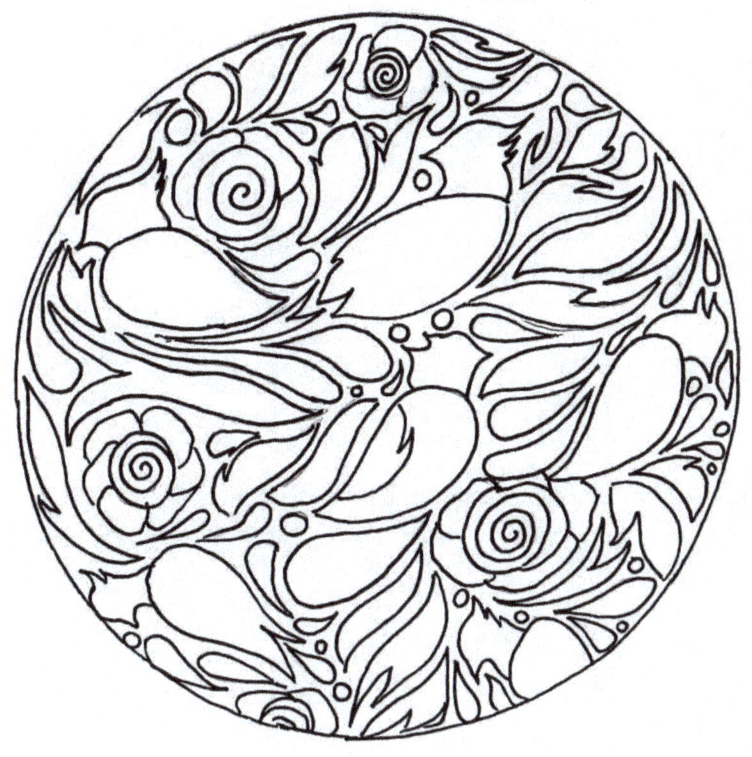

Cardinals and Flowers

by Richa Dinesh Sharma

Bold Brassy and beautiful

Danielle Martin

Beach Vibes

As bold as the sun blaring down,

on skin, salted by the clearest blue.

As daring as the young man

jumping off the emerald rock.

As gusty as the baby leatherback turtle

flapping its way into the frothy white

suspended above the sand,

the very sands, anchoring my feet.

So fearless, so determined.

I wish it could be me.

And the aww that builds within,

rivals any wave that spills.

Dipping Into the Past

I don't want to be like

that virgin image staring back,

photos tucked away in an expensive shoe box.

I want to do better.

I want to impact upon this earth,

even in places I've yet to step.

I can be better than the past,

better than the greed that caused so much pain.

It's funny - now - all this talk,

about holistic living and sustainability

when such was the way of the ancestors,

long before Columbus came.

No Matter Where You Are

Laden in the comforting hiss of a kettle

the cling and clang of cutlery

and the robust singing of tiny blue birds

that I can never see, even though I've tried,

is the remarkable knowledge that I am here.

It seems strange to acknowledge you're

not in the physical world,

for your laughter still fills the spaces shared.

You are part of the rising and setting of the sun,

part of the wind and rain

part of the moon and stars

no longer the picture

but rather the frame

always holding me in

holding me up

holding me,

even from afar.

Indy Samra

Shielded

My anxiety recoils and disowns me

I'm comforted with sensitivity

Wounds on my soul begin to heal

Savoring this moment, adoringly I close my eyes

Embraced and caressed reassuringly

Our heartbeats harmonised in their own rhythm

Each breath effortlessly coordinated

Desiring to remain here, at present and forevermore.

Invulnerable and shielded by you.

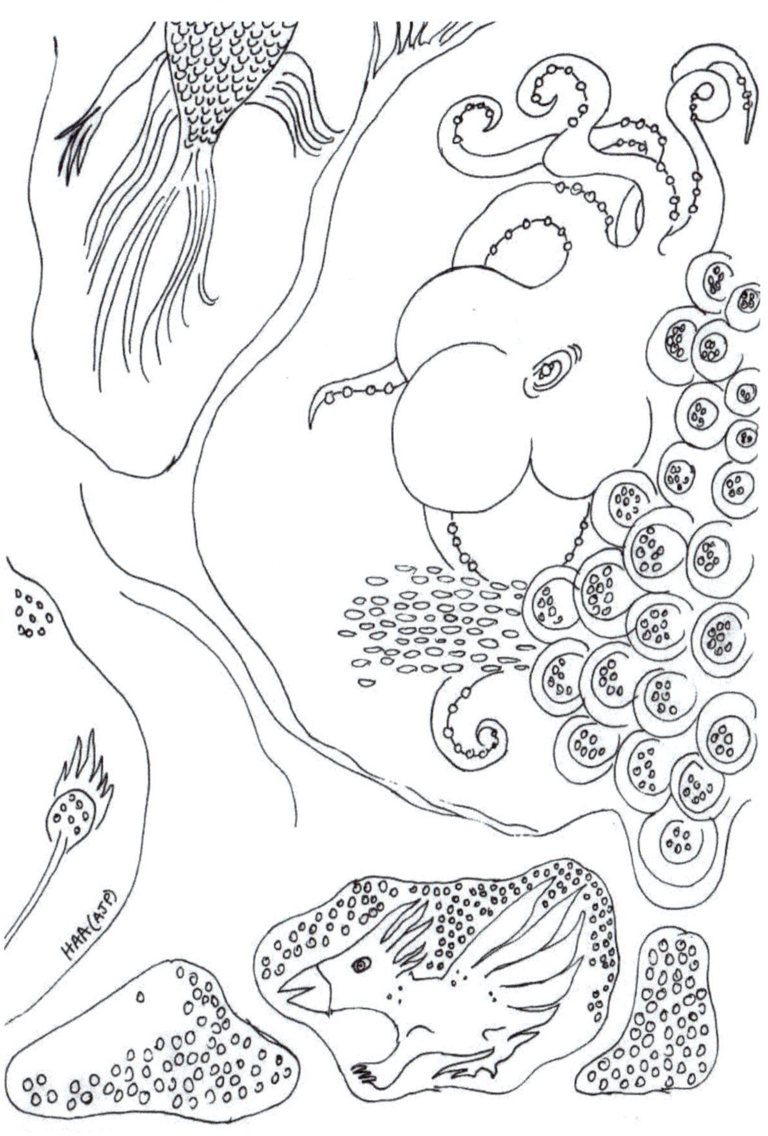

The Secret World by Heather Anderson

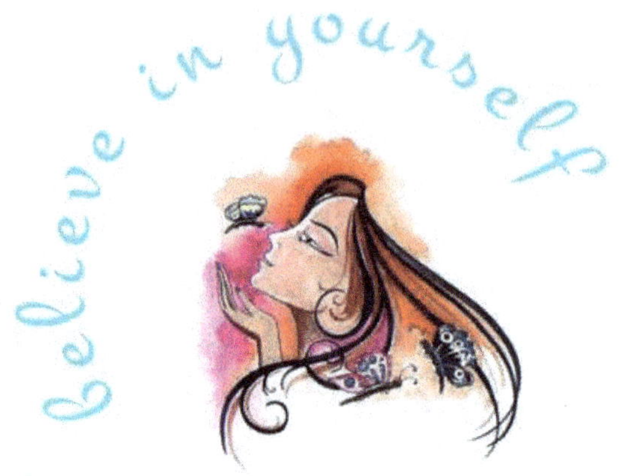
believe in yourself

Lauren Oertel

Passing on a Curve

I.
she gets in his car
chrome racing horse emblem
main source of his confidence
winding, the road narrows
but he's in a hurry
to show his prowess
slower cars in the way
grumbles of annoyance
he yanks on the steering wheel

she sees the truck in a flash—horn blasting
too late, throat screaming
tumbling down the mountainside
bucket seat unbolted
she ends up in the back
tongue bit in half
mouth streaming blood
femur fractured

he passed on a curve
she bears the scars

II.
life of the party
but only with Jack Daniel's in hand

two shots too many
promises he'll be fine
jokes he pushes over the edge
shoves another guy, who slams into her
her body flies, temple smacks the bar's corner
white towels soak up blood
six stitches

he passed on a curve
she wears the scar

III.
camping trip—
more of a hunting trip
his father's rifle
so old it likely wouldn't work
he grabs another beer
hands her the gun
just for fun, practice
old bullet jammed
in the chamber
trigger pulled—backfire explosion
gun powder, copper taste of blood
dripping from cheek gash

he passed on a curve
she carries her scars

but now she grabs the keys
and gets in the driver's seat

It's Not Too Late

If we do this, the possibilities abound, we change the
trajectory.
Gates guarding homes and neighborhoods, keep some out

Are they keeping out, or do they keep us locked in?
Security camera robots inform us that we're being recorded

We're being recorded as we walk along the sidewalk in
front of a house.
A house that suspects everyone, sees a threat in all of us,

We can relinquish the threat, replace the bars and cameras
with block parties.
Block parties where jars of cash collecting for a neighbor
in need go untouched

The cash sits in jars as the smell of grilling food swirls in
the air.
We make tacos fresh off the grill & with their screen-free
games, kids run amok

While the kids run, an unsupervised iPhone and speaker
provide
Background music until the band shows up. All throughout
the street,

Filling the street, our rhythm-connected bodies sway in a
shimmering wave
Of movement, flowing together to the sounds of liberation.

Anne Jennings Paris

The Night Canoe

Crescent-moon flickers in wind-tipped water.
The night canoe slips through drifts
of willow catkins. Swallows dart, swoop, retreat.
Frogs chirp from deep grasses, and a duck's flat honk
carries across the pond: everyone seeks a mate.

My paddle drips as I drift, listen, try to follow
shapes the willow makes where it touches
water. Every branch ends in a question:
which leaf is real, which reflection?
The falling dark brings keening,

stridulation. Forgive me. All this time, I'm still
a beginner, snarled in the knots of the past:
I tried wanting nothing, and it didn't work. Now
I want it all, and this is the only voice I've found.
If you didn't come to love me, turn around.

Artwork on page 113

Confession

I have not been seen.
I have not been given the love I thought I deserved.
The ones I thought were mine were not mine.

I reached out with my voice and received no answer.
I reached out with my voice and received an answer I did
not want.
I reached out with my voice and was shamed.

I hated a world that didn't know how to love me.
I hated myself for wanting to be loved.
I heard people tell me to love myself.
I didn't understand their words.

I reached out with my body and received no answer.
I reached out with my body and received an answer I did
not want.
I reached out with my body and was shamed.
I hated my body for being weak.

I knew a hundred people, and still I was alone.
I cried because there were no arms to hold me.
I tried to hold my sadness.
I got lost in my sadness.
No one came to save me.

Sometimes I want to leave my body: the work is too hard.
My fear swells until all I am is fear.
If I forget to breathe, my body breathes for me.

Artwork on page 109

To My Child Not Yet Born

I failed you before I was born.
You could not escape--
just as I could not unknow
the mother who cried in her bed,
the father I can't forgive.
Science tells us: You were formed
in the womb of your grandmother,
foretold, begotten, as I was, as I have been
clawing my way back to you every day since--
Yes, I have walked far to meet you,
every step a seeking:
May you be more than me.

Artwork on page 97

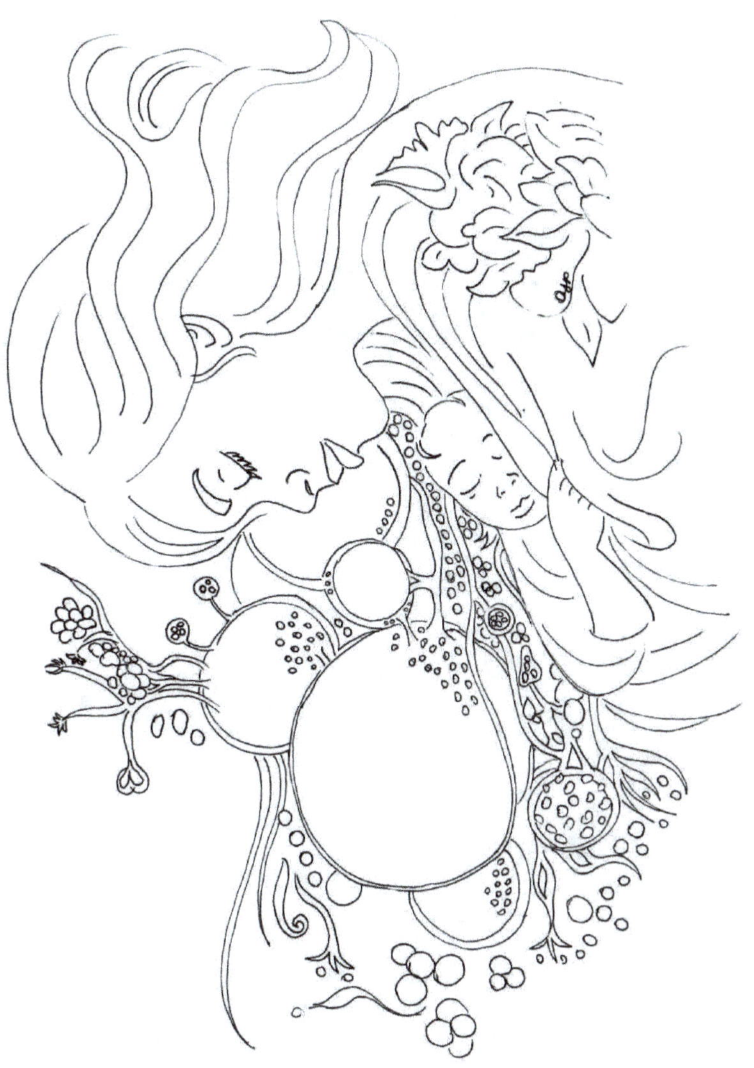

To My Child Not Yet Born
by Anne Jennings Paris

Poem on page 96

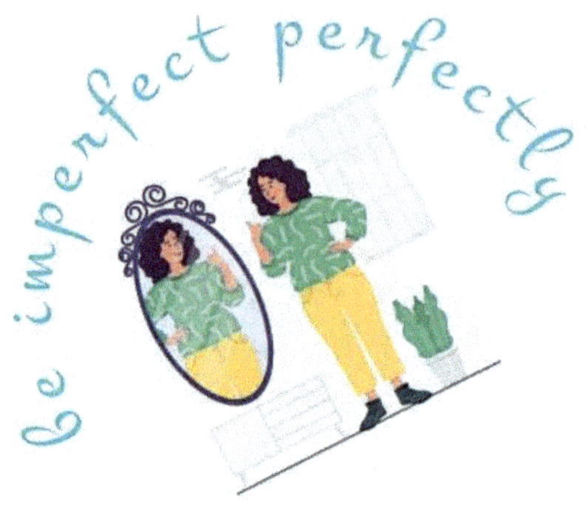

be imperfect perfectly

Reflection: Day 5

List three things that are causing you
stress or worry, then brainstorm
practical steps you can take to address
or alleviate each one

1. ....

....

....

2. ....

....

....

3. ....

....

....

Annette K Riddle

Putting a Song in My Heart

I remember coming to the Garden
Wondering if it would be a seasonal "when" -
A when of happening, of closed minds or closed doors,
Closing hearts, or much more in my scores -
A when somebody smiled in their eyes first
And as their smile from their cheeks burst forth
Their words more than welcomed, they wrote in my heart
Originality,
Homeopathy,
Home-type remedies of the heart's eyes to impart,
To me, of all people, I was to be gifted,
Along with all these other chosen,
Just by "walking in" be lifted.

I was so enthused, by the news,
To my ears, to my years,
That I congratulated myself on taking a step
To respond to the founder's letter left,
As an invite at another's sad closing,
To rise from the ashes, and bring some atoning,
Of sadness to wonder to joys met again,
Even more than before,
All because somebody thought of others more.

Persist, is what my mourning dove friend
And her friend, the sparrow sayeth,

Persist in your dreams, and what heaven does weighs in,
Your dreams are that heaven and human would somehow
combine,
And come to fulfill dreams for humankind,
And since sistership has a fulfilling role to play,
Why not take the moral my bird friends leave to mind,
Of forgiveness, and loyalty, and utter stick-to-it-ive-ness,
Till the love is paid forward, and not any less?

I now know what respect the space means,
I now know what respecting all the spaces means,
And that from all the space given to me,
And all the respect for me from me I gleaned.
Gleaned from cheeks bursting with tender soft smiles
Meant for my heart strings of memory's miles
Of buried goods and uncomfortableness, all the same thing,
In time now gently made to sing
From the Garden of Neuro's Book Club delish,
Book list this year - so good that I didn't resist.
Books that gave wondrous, astounding depths of meaning
To life's conundrums of my past forgotten times;
Healing me with participation and succor,
What more can a girl ask of any counselor?
More than a therapy group, I directed my future
From my present to thank my Garden sisters;
For in a therapy group, the client doesn't direct,
Yet here in the Garden, we have self-agency,
We learn, and live with such self-honoring respect,
We have new love and honor for each other always.

Who knew such a simple respect?
Sung in a song years ago,

Never astounded as it has to let go
Of early meanings to get at all the depths
Of beauty and wonder that we are to thee.
Beauty and wonder, what a treat;
Sung in a thunder, or even defeat;
Doesn't matter how, doesn't matter when,
The song I now sing, cause of the Garden and life in God,
then,
Is beauty and wonder, in my soul, and out to the world
again.

Little Moments Out to the World

There is Somebody I pray to
For when the little moments are overflowing;
And I fancy I see signs in Nature,
After a time of contemplation concerning.
There was the time a lone mourning dove,
Befriended by a sparrow,
Landed on the neighbor's fence,
With her friend in tow.
I didn't think much of it;
Until I saw them everyday –
Every season, every year,
Much to my imagined cheer.
For they were cheering me on,
A double light for my single going on.
Much to my relief,
A smile to repeat.
They'd fly everywhere together;
A news to write home from a favorite chair.

There was also the time,
Sad looks passed from our pets' eyes to mine.
There was nothing I could do,
So I looked at them forlorn and blue.
Trying to comfort in what ways I knew,
I just held them, and prayed,
To that Somebody I knew.

In good times, in fair,
Even worse times, He always cares.

Celebrations Close to Home

Half-awake, baby in my arms, safely snuggled in hospital
bed;
Nurse giving quick check-over, and call her if I need
anything.
I smirk, and think, she just gave me my light,
What could I possibly say as bright?
Instead, I say, okay, thanks.
We proceed to have Mommy and Daughter time
Rarest of all
First looks first smiles, first coos, first eyes
Tearing up from such emotion welling up.
Dad's first voice, take our picture, her and me.
Someone did, maybe me, sweet as can be.
And I asked for thea picture of her and myself.
Gave the pencil drawing of it to her as a Grandmom.
Loved every minute of raising her
Loved every minute of raising her brother
Even the scary parts – parts with no depth readings.
Just pass through, the other side is waiting.
Love every minute they give me of family life,
Maybe some more times I'll think up good types
Of stories and crafts, cookings and pets,
To walk, and play, talk and make,
And paint away, and sing away.

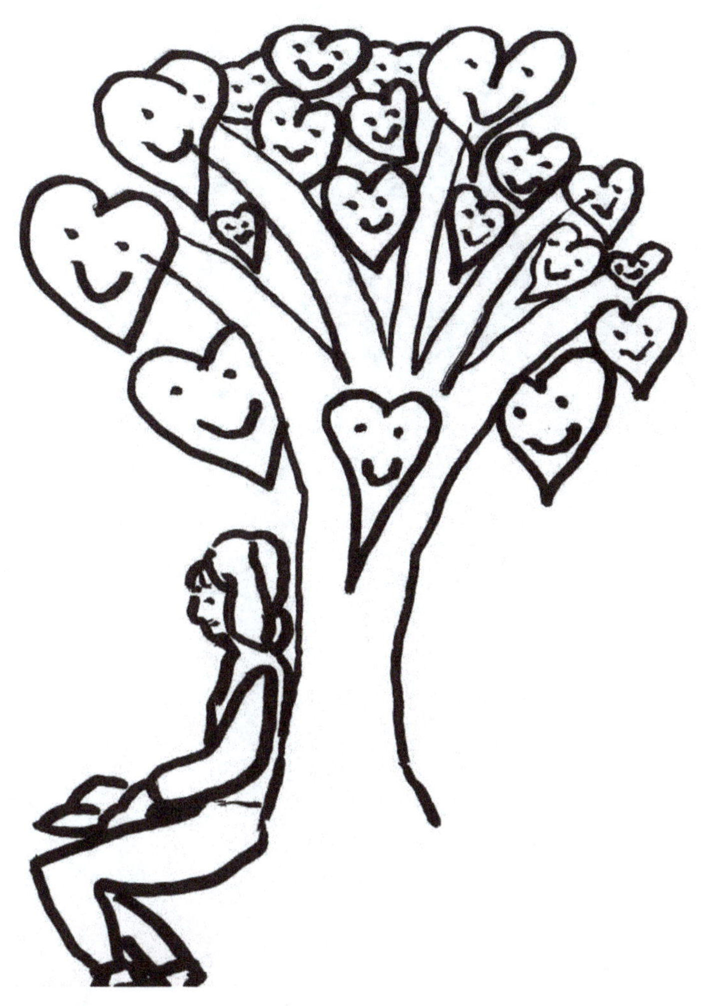

Annette Riddle

nourish the soul

Sarah Merritt Ryan

My Head Space

Breathe easy now

Settle and smile

My mind a clear haven

I can trust again.

Empty oasis open to new

No clutter or lingering fray

Core a tranquil, even plain

Ripe for planting dreams.

Believe in me I affirm

To love and embrace myself

Bravery and forgiveness takes

Humbling stance built upon grace.

Weariness ensues

Part of me quit long ago

But I awaken and fight

For the life I was granted.

Live my life now

Safe to be honest and express

With a sound mind I honor

And admire the resilience.

My worst enemy no longer

My sanctuary expands

My story speaks freely

Redeeming and true.

I am now one

Myself and no other

My own space secure

Safe and brave

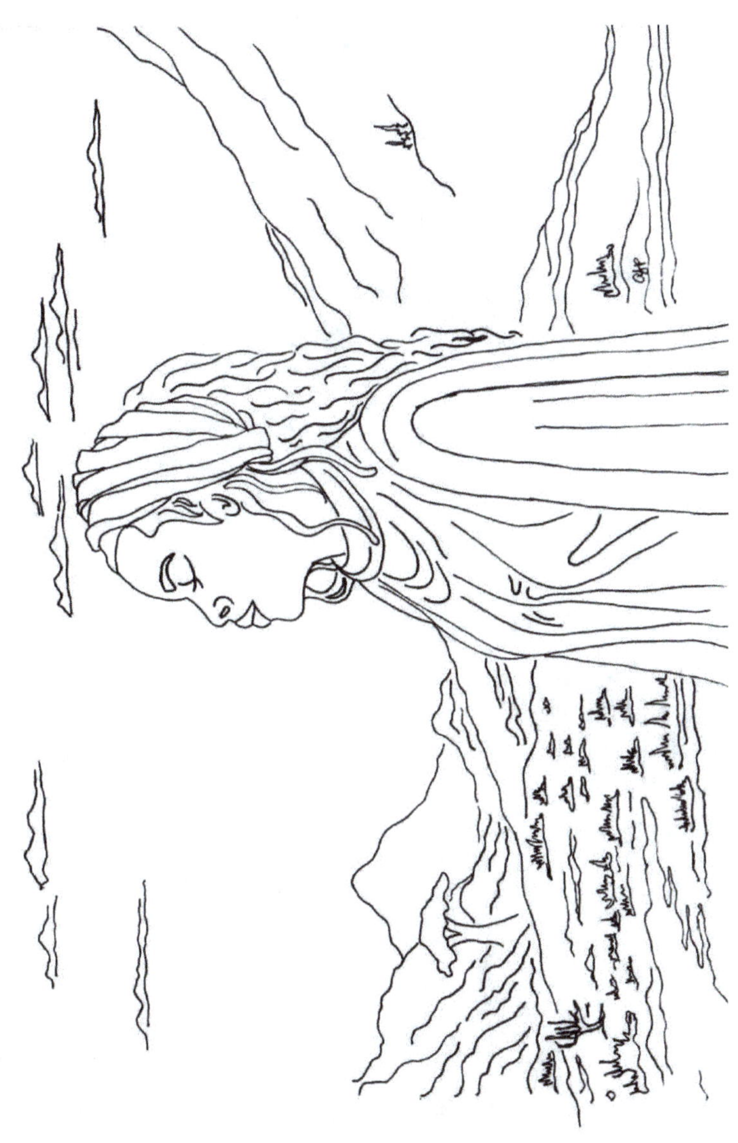

Confession by Anne Jennings Paris

Poem on page 95

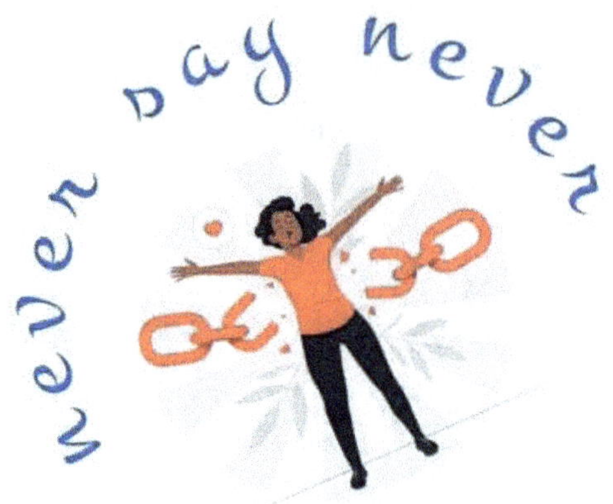

never say never

Lauren Salkin

Rainforest

in a melody
of raindrops
chirping creatures
vocalize
in a harmony of sound
breathing bountiful
nourishment
abiding
by the rules of nature
embracing waters
cool submersion
in aqua coated
streams
grasping sun-streaked
moments
slip through a canopy of trees
living in
hope
renewed
in seedlings birthed in the dirt
we grow

Autonomy

I accede to my feet
on a cushion, my relief
on the cusp of an afternoon
gray clouds gather in the distant blue

my mood imbued in a quiet moment
as shadows leave morning
on a misty green meadow
where a family is loved less

lost in willful ignorance
but I am free in my autonomy
in clouds I see float past trees
as summer's warmth transforms to fall

my floating thoughts search for peace
on this day, I acquiesce to me,
my needs, my dreams
foster my will to defeat

the chill that looms
in the still of winter
for which I will not waver in repose
my heart knows what is true

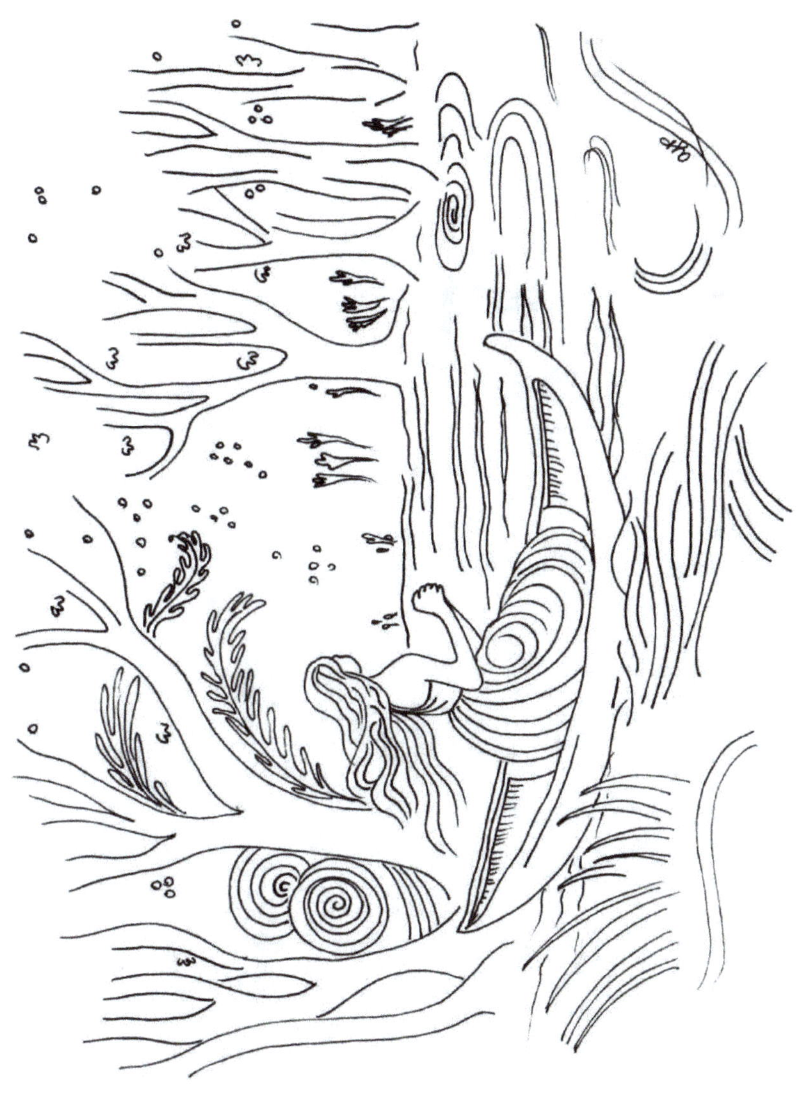

The Night Canoe by Anne Jennings Paris

Poem on page 94

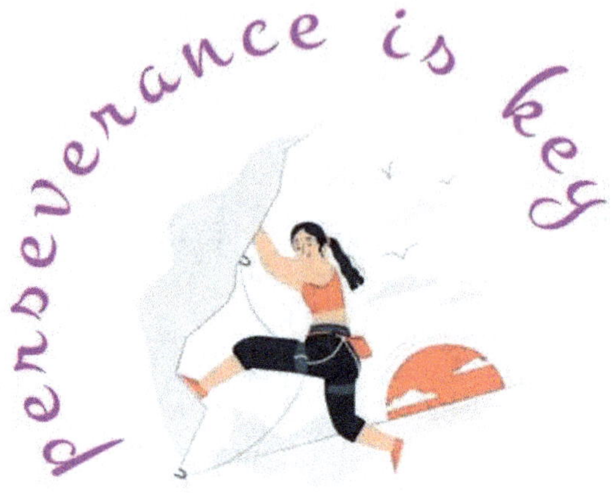

perseverance is key

Pratibha Savani

Flowers for the...

G reatness

A chieves

R esilience

D edication

E mpowerment

N oticeability

Outspoken and…

F ight

E ndure

A rise

R edefine

L ove

E nergise

S trive

S hine

AM I DREAMING?

I'm falling down a rabbit hole, gliding to a halt

Passing trees and a rainbow

I am already **Lost** in the magical world of **Oz**

The **yellow** brick road can't take me home

I'll have to ask the cheshire cat, which way to go

If I could go **Back to the Future**

Then my problems would be solved

But I'm trapped in a **Matrix**

Who has the key to get me out?!

To roll the dice like in **Jumanji**

And I would disappear

I need to find those ruby red slippers

To get me out of here!

Stranger things have happened

This is of course a world of magic

Supernatural powers exist

In a world of fairies and goblins

Could I be **Charmed**?

And wish me back home like Dorothy and Alice?

Or do I take the red pill and wake up?

Or be stuck having adventures **in Wonderland**?

Reflection: Day 6

Document your daily self-care rituals
and how they contribute to your
overall well-being, both physically and
mentally

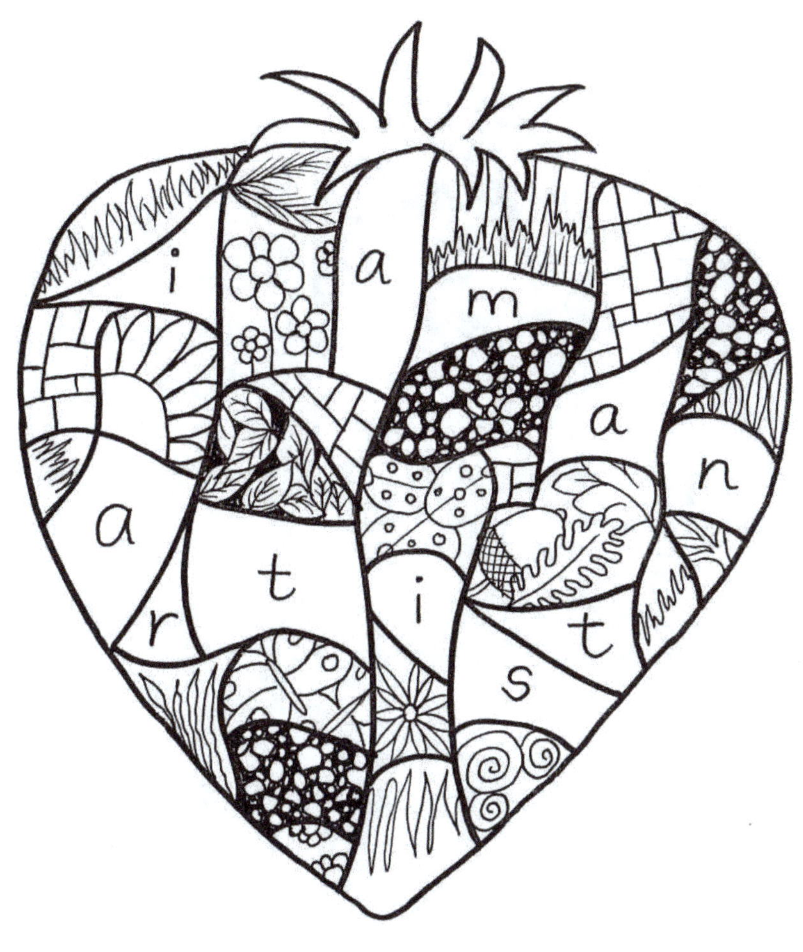

Strawberry Patch by Pratibha Savani

visualise your dreams

Shiela Denise Scott

Locked-In

Barricade me in a haven,

Where my art hangs on the wall,

No noise from others enters,

And my stands remain stood tall,

Cage me in my thoughts,

Where my books illustrate its content,

Designs of demonstration,

Have no barriers to resent,

Chain me to my goals,

Real purpose in life, which I need,

Keep me organized and aware,

A successful mind is how to succeed,

Uplift my spirits with exercises,

Daily affirmations and weekly chants,

About how perfection is becoming a habit,

And failure lost its circumstances.

Under the ground, I keep my secrets…

Beneath the grounded barriers,

Of the wounded at war,

I hide my secrets,

Ones known near and far,

Buried are the hurdles,

I had to overcome,

To keep safe my weakness,

And build strength from reality, succumb.

No longer will I be trustworthy,

Of those near to me,

Inconsistency isn't honest enough,

To present itself truthfully,

Don't dig up my lifestyle,

That left me behind,

Just leave it underneath,

Its RIP sign,

Respectfully.

Safe and Brave Space

I scream, as loud as I want too,

Its my place to be and become,

The one I wish to realize,

Everyone spited, or life a bit of,

I splash soap suds everywhere,

How I keep clean is my business,

No need to be comfortable with the worlds,

Filthy outer judgement,

It's my artistic realm,

The space known to none,

My purity,

My divinity,

My longevity of description of life for one,

Trinity,

Me, myself and I.

Anka Stanojčić

Live today

Don't waste new tears on old sorrows,
forget them, why are you sad,
While they think of some others,
days full of joy await you.

You only have today, yesterday is gone,
it will never come back like that again.
A better morning has come for you
and a day full of some new happiness.

Let everything sad be a lesson
so that it doesn't happen again!
You will meet some new people today
that your book is written with joy.

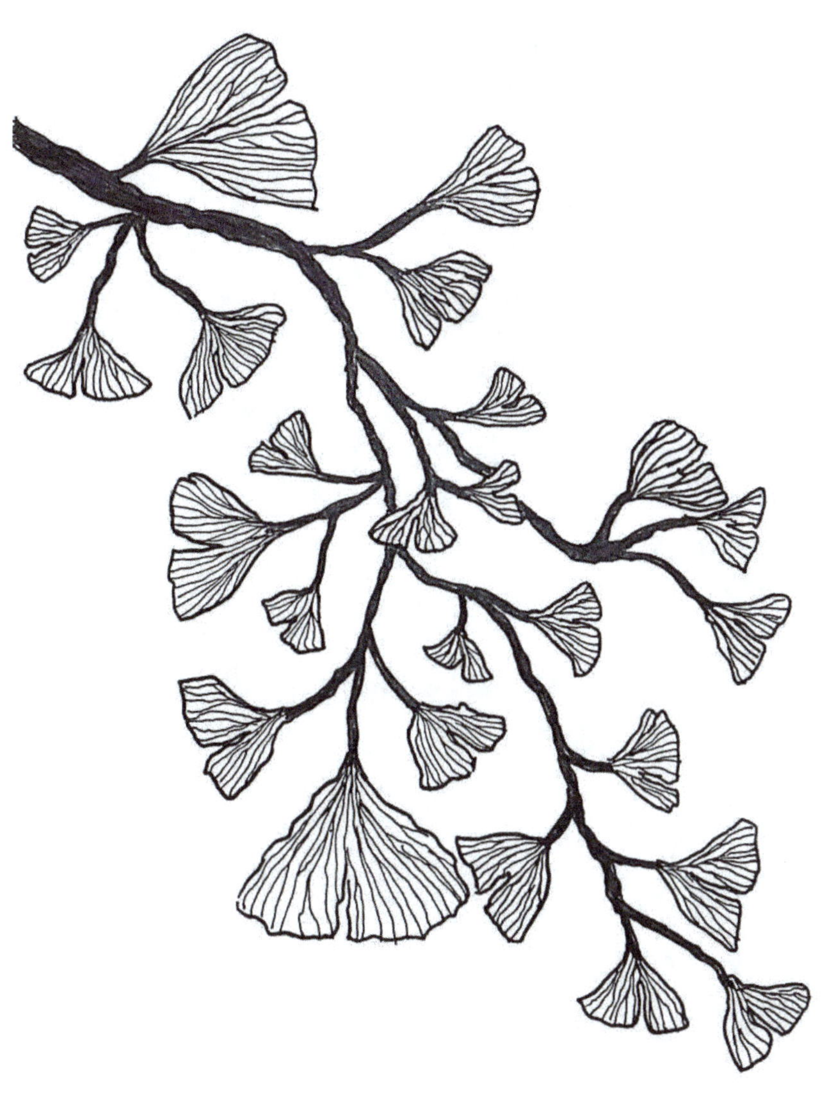

Gingko by Richa Dinesh Sharma

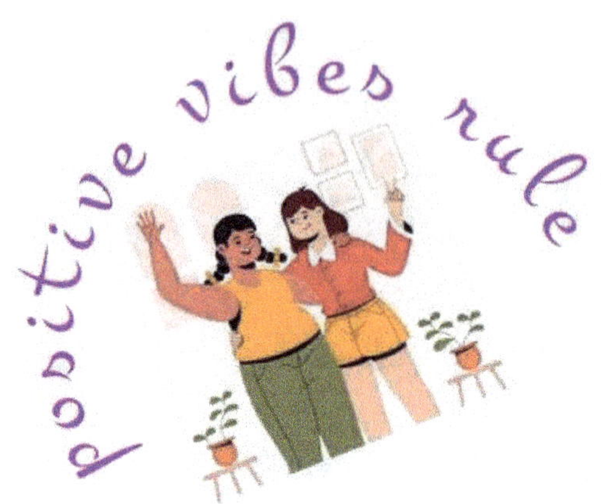
positive vibes rule

Richa Dinesh Sharma

I am a lost cause

Between choices, I lie and vacillate

like a pendulum that knows not to stop

I make up my own dreams

obstinately thinking them up

with my eyes closed

forcing my thoughts

to walk that line

and yet they digress

buzzing like gnats

I admonish them

dish out invisible swats

Reality scorches my throat

I die with each breath

when my dreaming takes a pause

and I dismantle in my own head

believing myself to be a lost cause

Louder Applause

Ever heard the sound of applause
It is like muted congenial lightening,
the thunderous joy of mortal gods
pulsing in waves across the room
shots of human energy to consume,
to enable the perfect synchronisation
of numerous beating human hearts
in harmonious, punctilious vibration
and palms are met over and over
in the claps of adrenaline high,
in the ridiculous scheme of things
a peremptory human action
of discreet inclusion of self
while offering ovation to others
keeping a few cheers to oneself

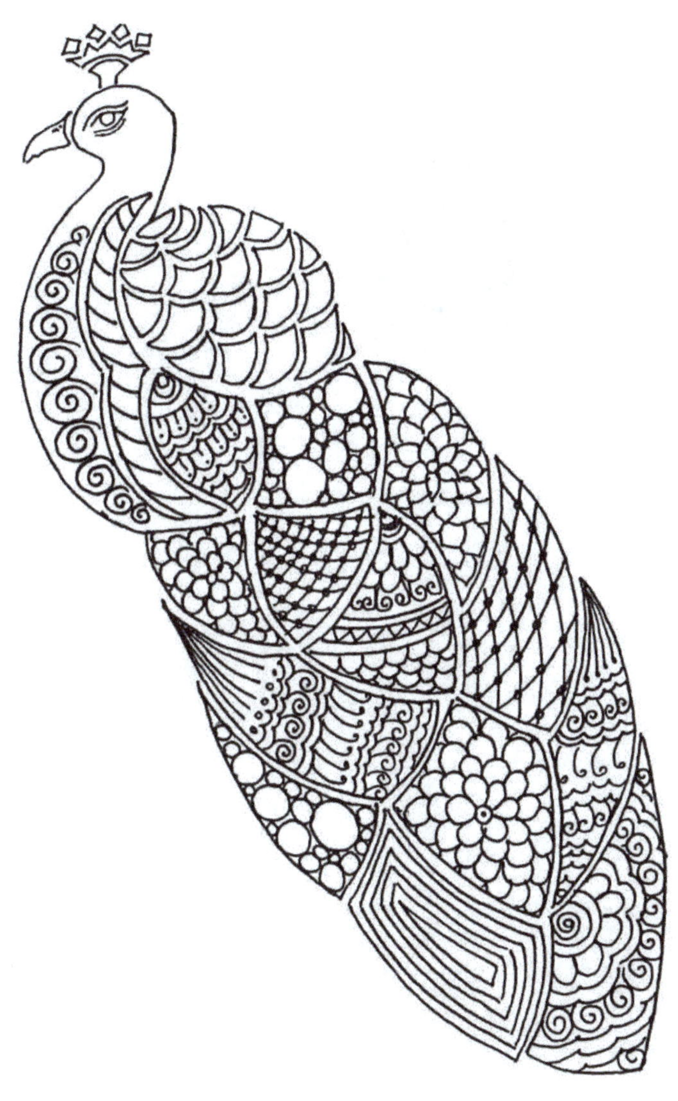

Peacock by Richa Dinesh Sharma

inspiring the world

Chanah Liora Wizenberg

Brave Space Safe? Space

Gather 'round,
circle up,
and listen well.

Important things
are about to happen.

This is sacred space.
It must be a *safe* space.

"How, you ask,
is this possible?"

Respect
Honor the author.
Don't make assumptions.

Refer to the narrator
not the writer.

Say what moved you.
Say what stayed with you.

Say what didn't work
so well, and why.

Remember you are about
to face the naked page.

There will be prompts
to choose from.

Pick one.
Begin to write,

birthing a new
poem, essay, or story.

Everything written
is to be considered fiction.

Unless the author
says otherwise.

There will be different
perspectives different
opinions.

Treat it like fiction
refer to the narrator

There will be different
experiences.

Some may be cultural.
Some may be religious.

Some may be political
All will be different

There may be
discomfort

Sit in the discomfort
Ask yourself, why?

It may it hit a nerve
sit with it some more.

Ask yourself, why?

Are your views being challenged?
Good

Important for you.
Focus on the writing.

What stayed with you?
What moved you?

School as Sanctuary

The doors were locked from the inside making
the assistant principal angry as hell.

Too bad, my students
come first.
Safety is key.
No bullies.
No bullying
permitted in
my classroom.
Ever.

Sensitive souls in the throes
of puberty are at work here
in this classroom.
My classroom.
A haven for *every* child.

Middle schoolers.
The ones I vowed I'd never teach
have taught me they are the most vulnerable group.
They need someone waiting for them when they arrive
home from school, or they may wail, "No one!" as one
child
did when asked, "Who cares for you at home?" That broke
my heart
and I wondered, how many others feel the same going
home to an empty house?

Home should be their primary haven.
When it is not, school can be, *should* be that safe place.
A sanctuary.

I made *sure* that my classroom was that place.

Brave is Breaking Boundaries, Making Waves and Standing Strong

She dresses in striking African attire
her head dresses of equal beauty complimenting
the days ensemble wrapped with intent with significance

She is the first in her family to go to college
they don't understand they shake their heads at her
not in disapproval but in the belief that she cannot achieve
the right, or stand in the light, in the way Maya Angelou
did
in the way that Gwendolyn Brooks did, in the way Nikki
Geovanni
and Rita Dove are doing and right behind them is Amanda
Gorman making
her own way forward no matter the odds

No, her family doesn't understand
they cannot see the potential or the possibility
of their daughter moving beyond or out of the projects

She ignores it all
she clings to her dream
every day she dresses with intent
chooses her headwrap to take strength
from her ancestors and to honor them walking
tall she pushes past the boys, the teens, the men who
knock the books out of her arms and try to pull her
headwrap

off and attempt to stomp her shoes
demanding to know why she is trying to be white
by daring to pursue advanced education

Gathering her books with one hand
while the other hangs onto her head piece
she will *not* be deterred, she to, walks like she
*"has oil wells in her living room"

I know her mantra must be, *"still I'll rise."
Maya Angelou would be proud

*From the poem by Maya Angelou, "I Rise."

Lisa Tomey-Zonneveld

Dance, Dance

Dancing was big in our family

our parents loved to dance on weekends

at the NCO club, sometimes taking us,

they were like Fred Astaire and Ginger Rodgers

as they slid over the floor, feet lit on clouds,

gazed stars in each other's eyes—

They star danced to melodies,

captured what they needed,

flickers started into flames.

We were born like stairsteps into a new season.

Their love journeyed on, into each other's arms.

Dance, dance, let your shiny black shoes glow

as you bounce to the tunes

as your dress and suit coat flow

Dance, dance, let your eyes catch the gaze

as the night moved on into the golden haze.

Let us dance.

When Suicide Was Not the Better Choice

I have a book on my shelf that is of all the poems one
woman wrote
and then she died—
suicided they called it—
but there is so much in the book to indicate the more
what is provoked in me is the more—
let down by society, social awareness is only good if it
matters
if something is done about it
not to worry, just let someone else deal with it
there are other unfortunate souls in this earth
it's a sad lot, but what to do—
what to do—
in a free country, i expect more
the more that saves lives
the more that provides for basic, essential needs
the more that keeps mothers sane
the more that keeps children from orphanhood

society sucks the life out the essential blood filled vessel
so it can cushion another congressional pew
so it can grease the hands of shifty politicians
so it can actually cause any of them to just look you in the
eyes and say "so."
once, a politician was invited to hear women talk about
their challenges
help them raise their children, attend to their basic needs

provide an education and a safe roof over their heads
said politician said they would be there to listen
said politician was a no-show
said politician was hunted down
said politician showed up for the meeting
the women had their say
who knows if it mattered to the politician
but it mattered to the women to be heard
it was not that night; it was the power past that night
when they helped each other with childcare, food,
transportation
to get to the point where they could go to the ballot box
and vote

Daddy

From the time I was tiny, I sat by daddy's side

a dent he'd call it from my close snuggles

the sun turned to daddy's desires

so did we.

Daddy was my safe person, along with mom.

They always willed to do their best.

It made me want to be a good girl.

Daddy and I share a certain delight—

ice cream could happen every single night.

Daddy called it medicinal.

I believed it had superpowers.

Our other shared delight was cookies.

I learned to bake his favorite cookie treats.

The one that he loved the most, I want to share.

Perhaps you have a parent, loved one, friend

who needs some sweet tooth cheer.

There's something to be said about sweet tastes.

Soft Sugar Cookies

Daddy's Favorite, especially if I added chocolate chips

Preheat oven 425° F

Grease cookie sheets

Ingredients:

3 ¼ cups flour

1 teaspoon soda

½ teaspoon salt

½ cup soft butter

1 cup sugar

1 egg, unbeaten

1 teaspoon vanilla

½ cup sour cream

Stir together flour, soda, and salt

In a mixing bowl place:

Sugar, butter, egg and mix at medium speed, about 2 minutes.

Add sour cream and the dry mixture to mixer ingredients and beat just until well blended.

Roll out on a floured surface to about ¼ inch.

Cut and sprinkle with sugar.

Put on prepared cookie sheets.

Bake for 12 minutes or until golden.

Make about 2 ½ dozen cookies.

Reflection: Day 7

Imagine your day from start to finish, incorporating activities and practices that nourish your mind, body and soul. Now jot down actionable steps to bring elements of that day into your life regularly

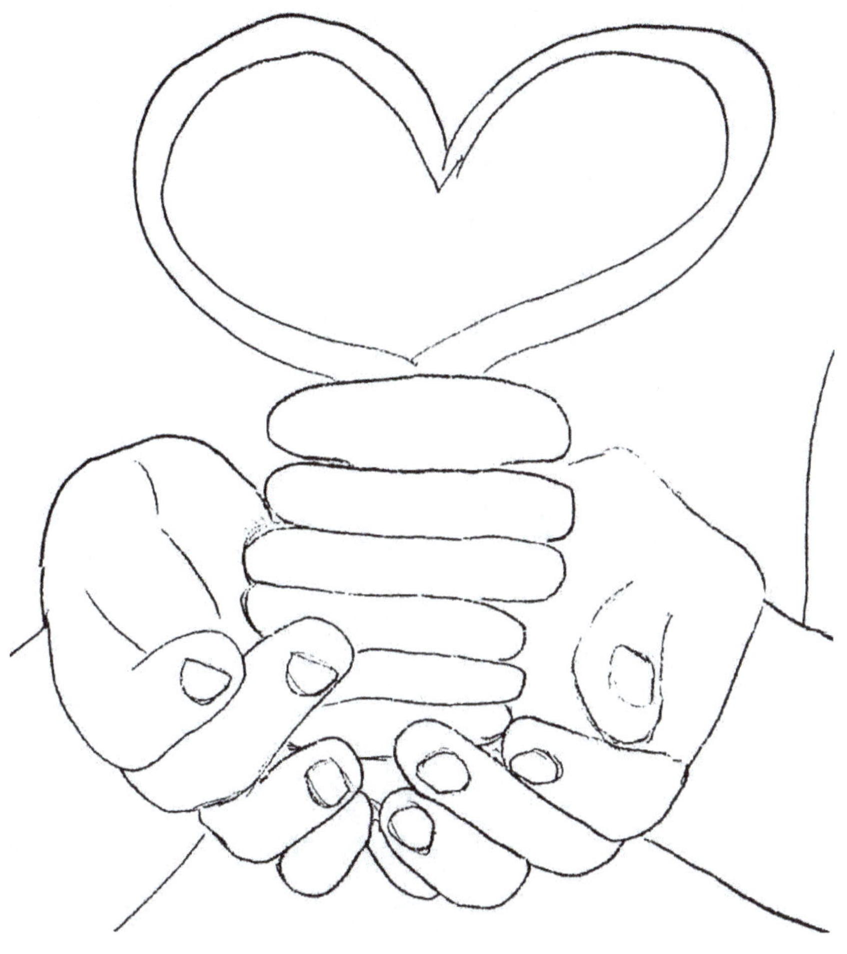

Sugar Cookies by Lisa Tomey Zonneveld

Recipe on page 142

imagine the possibilities

Biographies

Heather Anderson

Art educator and painter Heather Anderson intertwines her passion for teaching with exploring surrealism and biomorphic designs. With a palette that mirrors the whimsy of dreams and the complexity of nature, Heather's artistic journey becomes a living canvas, inspiring students and enthusiasts alike to embrace the limitless realms of creativity.

Tanja Ajtic

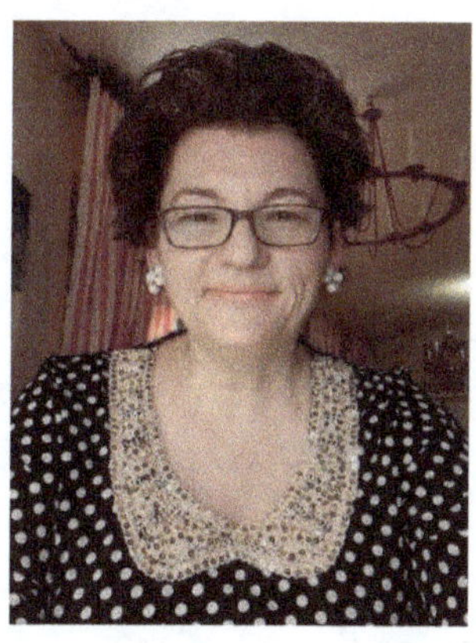

From Serbia and Canada, Tanja is a poet, writer and a freelance artist. Her poems have been published in 200 collections, anthologies, and magazines in eleven languages. She has published a book of poetry "Contours of Love" 2018. She is the winner of many awards and diplomas. She does artistic graphics that have been published in books, magazines.

Nanci Arvizu

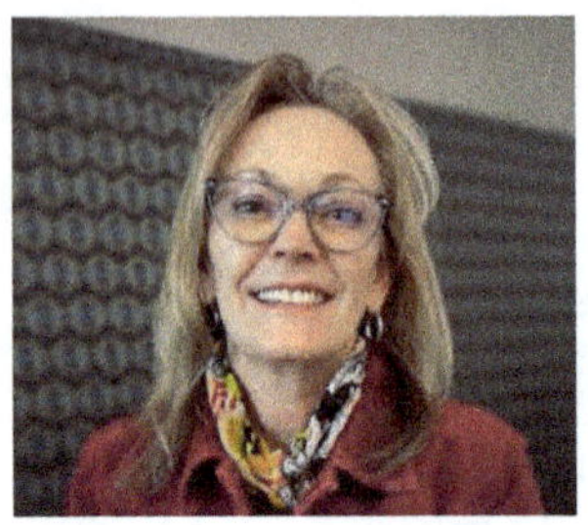

Nanci Arvizu, a published author, ghostwriter, editor, and interviewer, transforms ideas into published works. Recognized as a thought leader in business development, operations, and project management, she is a dynamic achiever. Beyond the writing realm, Nanci is a Peloton enthusiast, avid hiker, globe-trotter, budding poet, one-time songwriter, and captivating public speaker. Her diverse talents mirror a journey from concept to creation, making her a beacon in the literary and entrepreneurial landscapes.

Arlene S Bice

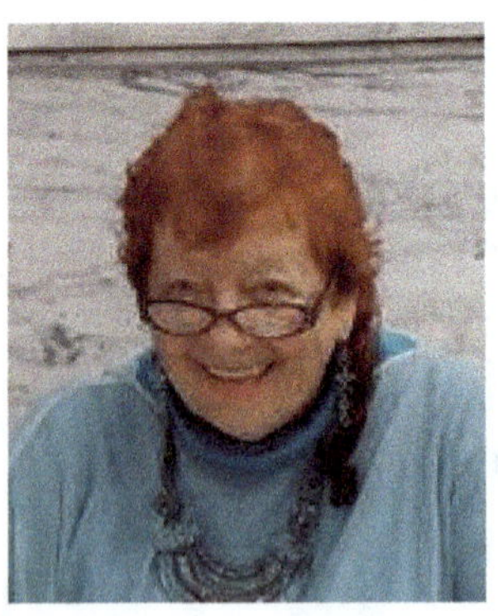

Arlene s Bice is the recipient of the Florence Poets Society Poet of Distinction Award and Annual Literary Oakley Hall Award. Her poetry is published in several anthologies. She lives in Farmville, Virginia. Her books are available on Amazon.

Natalie Bisso

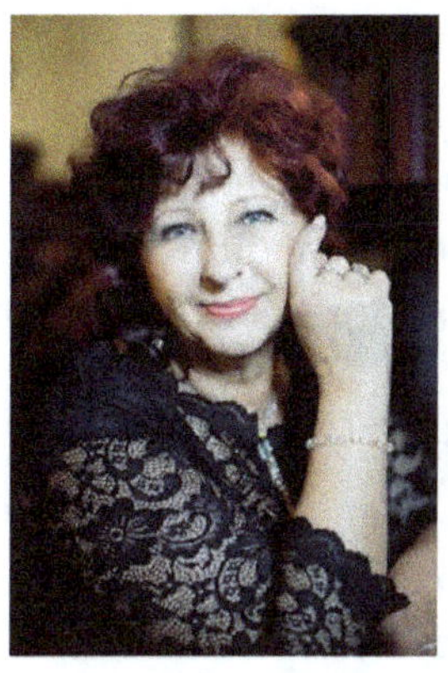

Natalie Bisso is a poet, novelist, essayist, and songwriter. Author of 13 collections of authors, co-author in more than 180 international collections. The poems have been translated into 40 languages and published in international anthologies. Honorary Figure of World Literature and Arts with the award of a silver badge. Takes part in the literary life of different countries.

Yasmin S. Brown

Yasmin S Brown is an international bestselling co-author, poet, certified life coach, and Guinness World Record participant. Developing her leadership and public speaking skills in Toastmasters International ultimately achieving her DTM (Distinguished Toastmaster). Yasmin utilizes her personal and healthcare professional experience to advocate for women's mental health. Through innovation, she brings organizational health, communication, and trauma-informed awareness.

Lin Marshall Brummels

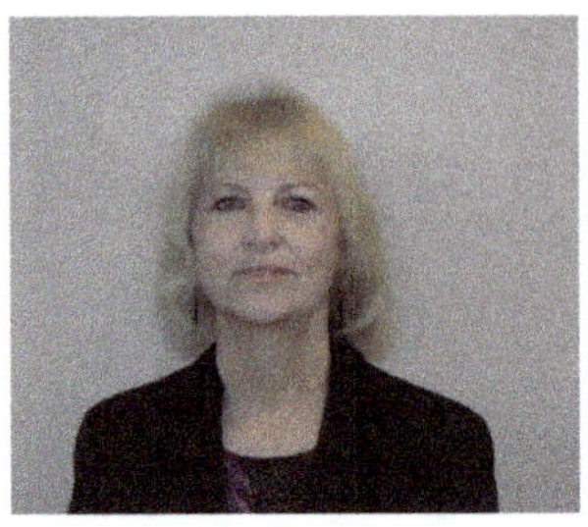

Lin Marshall Brummels earned a BS from the University of Nebraska and a MS from Syracuse University. "Jerry's Hands" was selected as an Honorable Mention poem in the 2021 Nebraska Poetry Society's contest. Brummels has poems in *Poet Lore, San Pedro River Review, Concho River Review, Oakwood, Plainsong, Nebraska Life,* and others. Her chapbooks are "Cottonwood Strong" and "Hard Times," a 2016 Nebraska Book Award winner. Books: "*A Quilted Landscape,*" *Scurfpea Publishing.* Forthcoming, *The Last Yellow Rose,* from Sandhills Press.

Joni Karen Caggiano

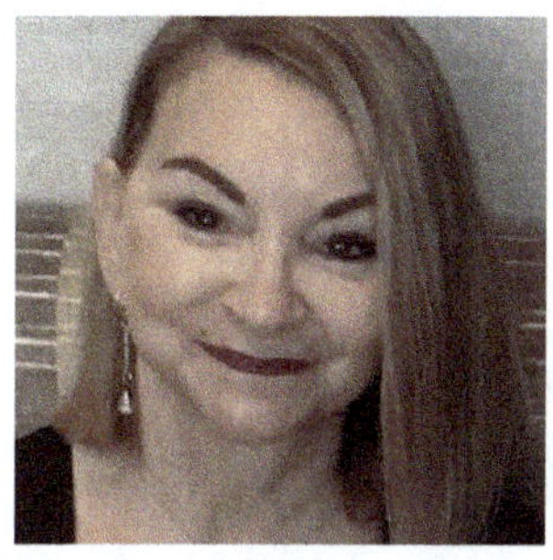 Joni is a Pushcart Nominee for 2022, an internationally known and published poet, photographer, author and co-author of the Amazon #1 bestselling poetry anthologies "Wounds I Healed: The Poetry of Strong Women," and "Hidden in Childhood, A Poetry Anthology." She is a regular contributor to MasticadoresIndia, MasticadoresUSA, HotelMasticadores and Spillwords Press NYC, twice nominated and won Publication of the Month for "Love Me Like a Luna" (November 2022). 2023 Co-Winner of "Socialite of The Year." Joni shares her story as a surviving Adult Child of Alcoholics (ACOA) in her blog, "Rum and Robots." Joni's blog is an effort to help other ACOAs through faith and a strong kinship with nature. Joni is a retired nurse.

Vanessa Caraveo

Vanessa Caraveo is an award-winning author, published poet, and artist whose literary work brings focus to various social issues that exist today. She has been published in *Literature Today Journal, The Poet Magazine, Latinidad Magazine, Poetrybay, Anacua Literary Arts Journal,* and in multiple anthologies throughout the years.

Jeri Day

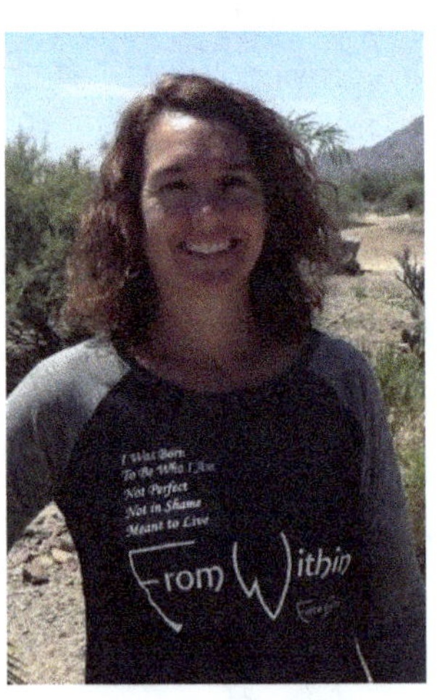

Jeri Day lived life with grace, humor, and purpose. She loved writing, her two beautiful children, animals big and small, and helping others in need. She held a Bachelor's Degree in Psychology and was poised to change the world when she suffered a Gran Mal seizure and passed away in 2019. She is still greatly missed.

Anna Ferriero

Anna Ferriero, an esteemed Italian poet, earned WNWU membership in 2019 and an honorary doctorate in 2020. As an IFCH member since 2022, she was appointed the International Ambassador of Peace in 2023 for India and Bangladesh. A Naji Naaman Literary Prize winner in 2020, Anna is renowned for her collections like "Magia d'Amore" and "Punto, Oltre l'Orizzonte." She's a prolific editor, translator, and recipient of numerous national and international awards, including the Journalistic Grand Prize for Social Merit in 2023. Her influence extends globally through translations and collaborations, representing Italy in Turkey's Guncel Sanat.

Nolcha Fox

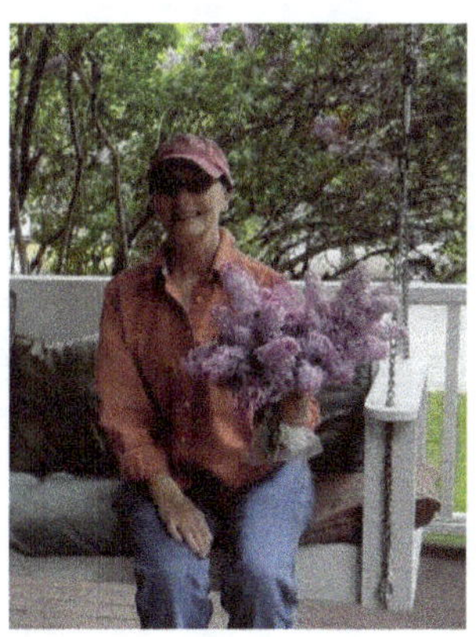

Nolcha Fox's poems have been curated in print and online journals. Her poetry books are available on Amazon and Dancing Girl Press. Nominee for 2023 Best of The Net. Editor for Open Arts Forum, Chewers & Masticadores, Garden of Neuro. Accidental interviewer. Fake news faker.

Garden of Neuro Institute Poet Laureate, 2024

Lisa Hartsgrove

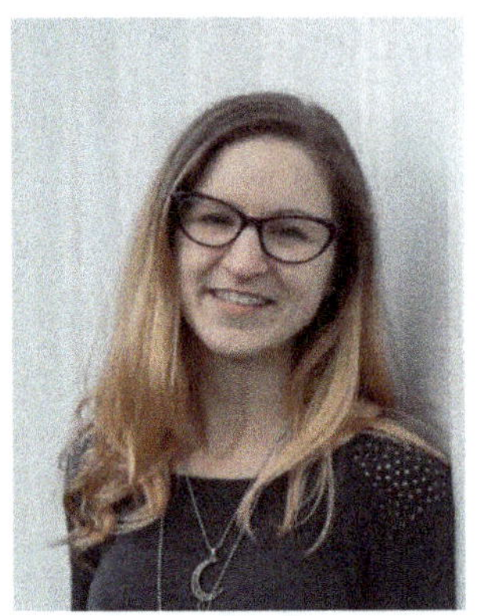

Lisa Hartsgrove is program coordinator & writing instructor for Project Write Now, a nonprofit transforming individuals, organizations, and communities through writing. She has been published in *The Pitkin Review*, *Collage*, and The Atlantic Highlands' "Herald." She also took first place in the 2019 Laury Egan HBAC Poetry Contest and third place in the 2014 Jersey Bayshore Writing Contest. Lisa is currently working on a YA novel-in-verse as well as keeping up with a daily "One Sentence a Day" writing project she began in March of 2016. You can read more at lisahartsgrove.com.

Tina Hudak

Tina Hudak lives, studies, and works in the Washington, D.C. metropolitan area since moving here in 1975 from her hometown of Bethlehem, PA. Her early training in calligraphy led to apprenticeships as a hand papermaker, book artist, and writer. She continues her artistic endeavors through several organizations and their programs, and creates pieces seen on *A Blue Bunny Studio* on Wordpress. Her art is in collections at the Harvard College Library (MA), and The Library of Congress (DC) among other institutions including private collections. In addition, her poetry books reside at the Library of Congress, Enoch Pratt Free Library (Maryland's State Library) with individual pieces published through Indie presses online and in print.

Chyrel J. Jackson

Chyrel J. Jackson is a Literary visionary and #1 Ranked Best Selling Amazon Author. Reared and raised in the South Suburbs outside Chicago. In the Summer of 2022 Chyrel was a contributing writer in the #1 Best Seller ranked Anthology "Not Just Anybody Can Be Dad."

Previously published Mirrored Images and *Different Sides of the Same Coin. Chyrel's writing appears in multiple published* poetry Anthologies and Literary Journals. You will find her always writing. Creating written legacies one book at a time.

You can find her on Sistersrocnrhyme.com

Alison Jennings

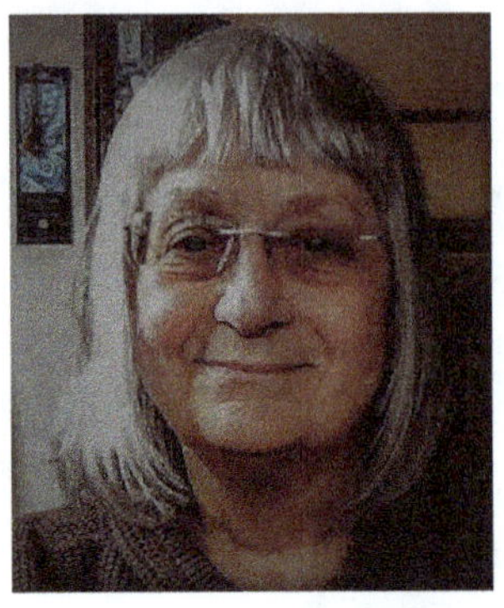

Alison Jennings is a Seattle-based poet who taught in public schools before circling back to her first love, poetry. She's had a mini-chapbook and 80 other poems published in numerous journals, including *Amethyst Review*, *Mslexia,* *Poetic Sun, Stone Poetry,* and *The Raw Art Review*, plus winning 3rd Place/Honorable Mention in several contests.

Katarina Jurčevic

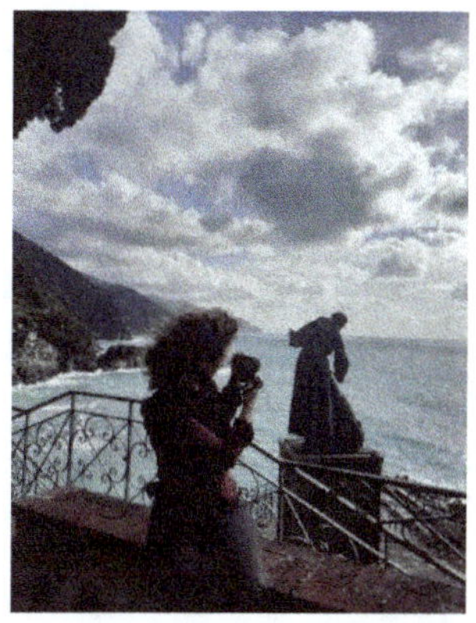

Katarina Jurčević was born in 1999 in Zaječar, Serbia. She currently lives in Belgrade where she attends the Faculty of Philology, University of Belgrade, majoring in General Literature and Theory of Literature. She is a member of the Society of Serbian Women Writers. Her poems have been published in literary journals in Serbia like Enheduana, Suština poetike. In the proceedings Touch of Japan, Šraf 9/2022, Ljubav u jesen, Cry of a Woman: Mother of the Earth, In the Embrace of Eternity: 50 Years Since the Death of Milunka Savic. Her stories were published in the proceedings: Neko je pritisnuo dugme, Čas prirode. She is the winner of the First Prize at the Belgrade Story Competition: The Belgrade Museum of Stories for the Story Kalemegdan.

Zaneta Varnado Johns, with Kyla Y. Cooper, and Kyli L. Cooper

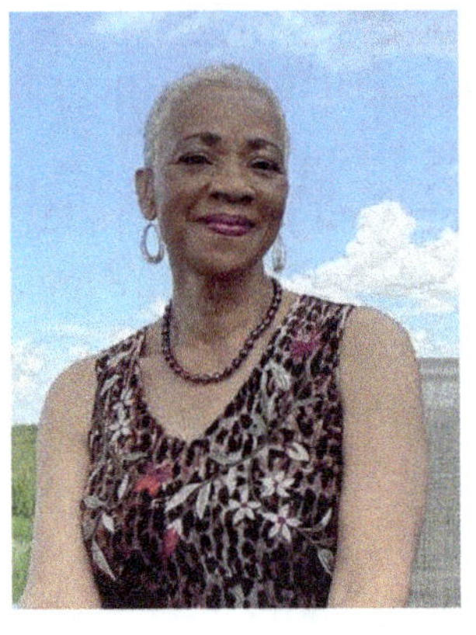

Zaneta Varnado Johns is a Pushcart Nominee in Poetry and 4-time bestselling author of *Poetic Forecast*, *After the Rainbow*, *What Matters Journal*, and *Encore*. Johns is a co-author in the Women Speakers Association's #1 international bestsellers *Voices of the 21st Century* (2021, 2022, 2023). Her poems are featured as the Dedication page in these collaborative books. Johns resides in Colorado, USA. www.zanexpressions.com

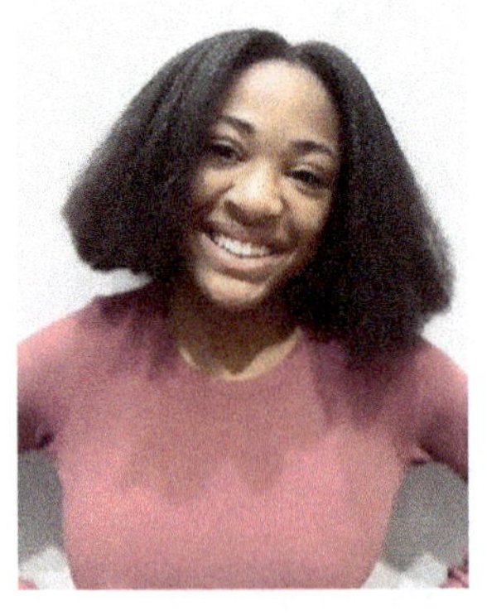

Kyla Y. Cooper is a gifted eight grader whose life is meant to be. Born three months early, she is a testament to the power of prayer. She is an award-winning competitive cheerleader whose team won a national championship in 2023. Kyla is a visual artist who also creates miniature crafts. She and her miracle twin Kyli are members of their Rogers, Arkansas cheer squad.

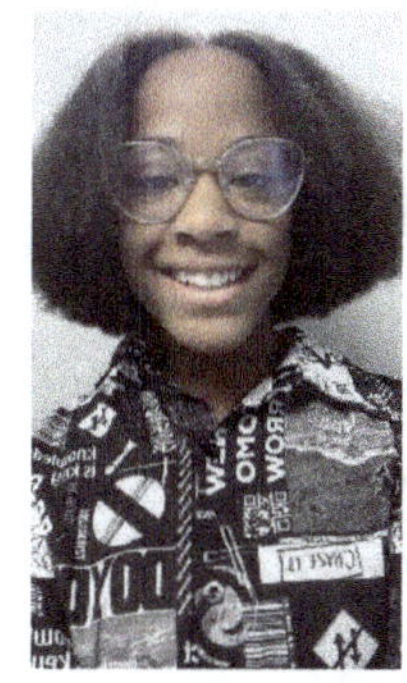

Kyli L. Cooper is a multitalented eight grader whose life is meant to be. Born three months early, she is a testament to the power of prayer. She is an award-winning gymnast, singer, and visual artist, among other things. She and her miracle twin Kyla are members of their Rogers, Arkansas cheer squad.

Jill Sharon Kimmelman

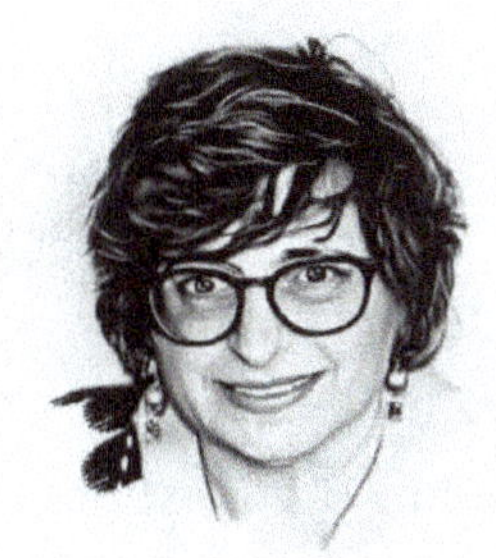

Jill Sharon Kimmelman is a two-time Pushcart Prize nominee in Poetry, She regularly contributes to internationally themed anthologies and literary publications. Her debut poetry/art book, "You Are The Poem", was released in November 2021. She is working on her second book. Jill lives in Delaware, USA with her husband Tim Little. She is the proud mother of her son Jordan.

Robin Klammer

In a nutshell, author Robin Klammer is a forlorn mid-life writer gal, from Western Canada who is writing a brand new chapter in her story. Robin loves live music, nature, animals, and great friends! Writing is her way of offering a smile or hope to people when they need it most.

Barbara Leonhard

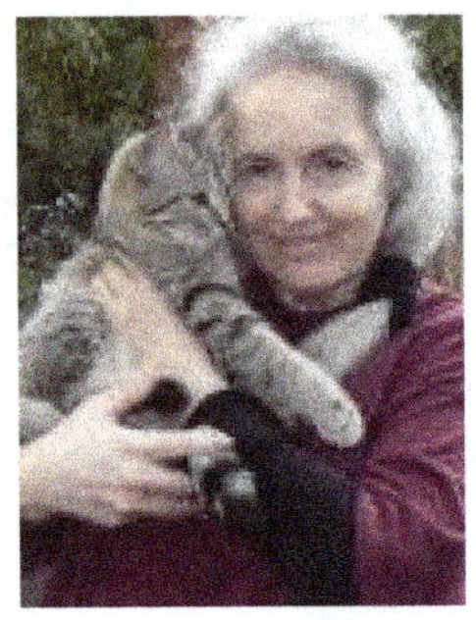

Barbara Leonhard is a retired ESL instructor. Since retiring, she has written a poetry collection *Three-Penny Memories: A Poetic Memoir* (Experiments in Fiction, 2022), which is about her relationship with her mother, who suffered from Alzheimer's. Barbara is also the Editor for MasticadoresUSA. She lives in Mid-Missouri with her husband and cat Jasper.

Danielle Martin

Danielle Martin is a Former Caribbean Journalist and Copywriter turned poet, her debut poetry collection, **Kissing Shadows: Caribbean Love Poems,** and a short story collection, **Sweet Talk: Caribbean Culture** are available on Amazon.

Danielle's poetry and art graced the previous edition of A Brave and Safe Space, and she is thrilled to be a part of this project once again. Her work can also be found in several international poetry anthologies and online publications.

Follow her on Facebook @DanielleM

Preeti Mistry

Preeti Mistry, a visual artist and designer, draws inspiration from pattern, shapes, and forms. She specialises in crafting free-flowing artwork, captivating mandalas, intricate black and white pen drawings, and mesmerising dot paintings. In addition to her artistic pursuits, she explores paper quilling, jewellery crafting, and specialises in floral designs. Discover her work on instagram @preeti_little_things and @preetiflowers.

Lauren Oertel

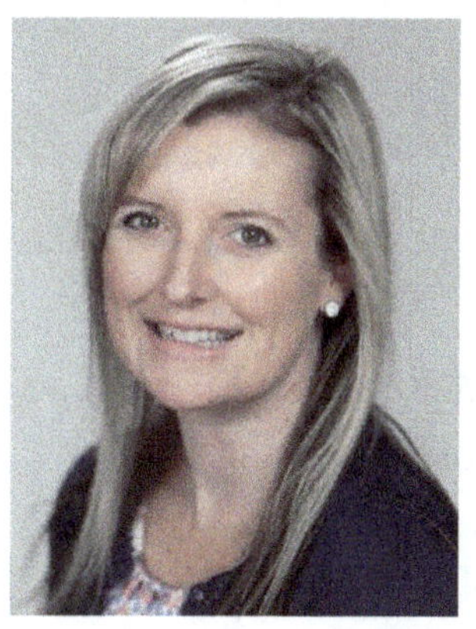

Lauren Oertel is a community organizer covering Texas and New Mexico for a nationwide nonprofit. Her work has been published in The Ravens Perch, Evening Street Review, The Bloom, Steam Ticket, Gemini Magazine, Last Stanza, Mystic Owl Magazine, Noyo Review, MONO., and The Sun Magazine. She lives in Austin, Texas, with her partner Orlando and their tuxedo cat Apollonia.

Anne Jennings Paris

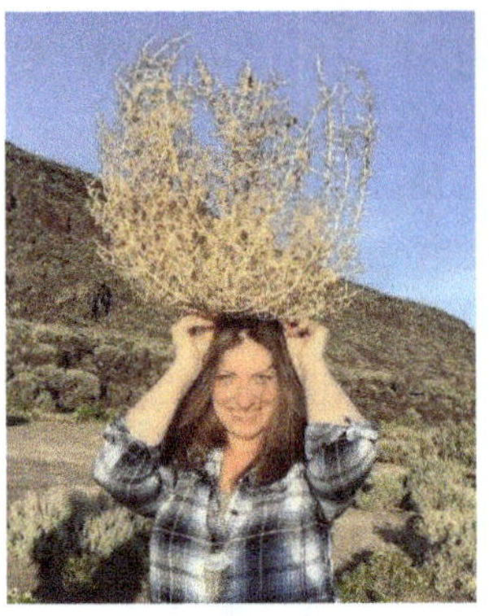

Anne Jennings Paris is a writer and artist living in Portland, Oregon. Her book-length collection of poems, *Killing George Washington*, was nominated for an Oregon Book Award. She has taught writing at San Jose State University, Portland Community College, and the University of Portland; and been writer-in-residence at Everglades National Park and Playa Center for the Intersection of Art & Science.

Annette K. Riddle

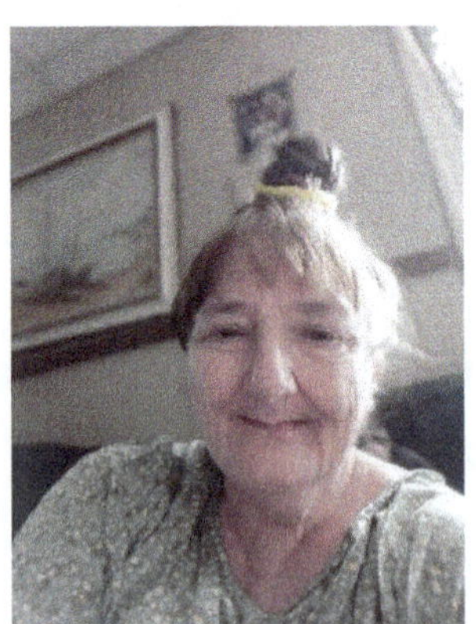

A Michigander, Annette's heritage is from St. Joseph, Ontario, Canada, and Bardstown, Kentucky, plus dreams of heaven. She only dabbled in poetry at various times of her life until coming to the Garden of Neuro in January 2023. Lisa Tomey-Zonneveld inspired her at a poetry workshop, resulting in over 150 poems.

Lauren Salkin

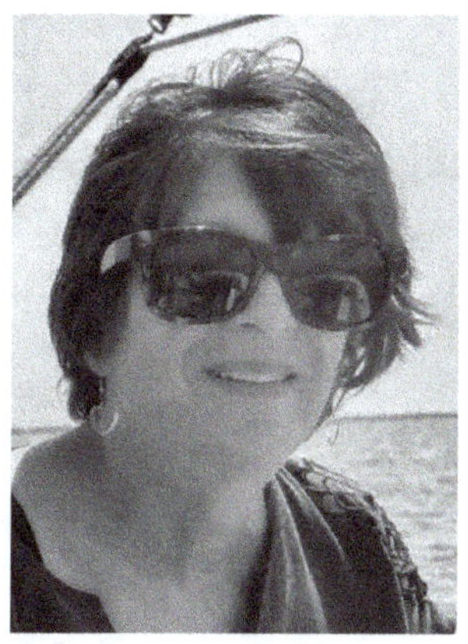

Wife, mother, & loser of stuff. Making sense out of chaos. Writer of humor, satire, poetry, and thought pieces. Published work has appeared online and in print. Huffington Post, Extra Newsfeed, Literally Literary, Muddyum, The Haven, as well as ByLine, and Shroud Magazine.

Sarah Merritt Ryan

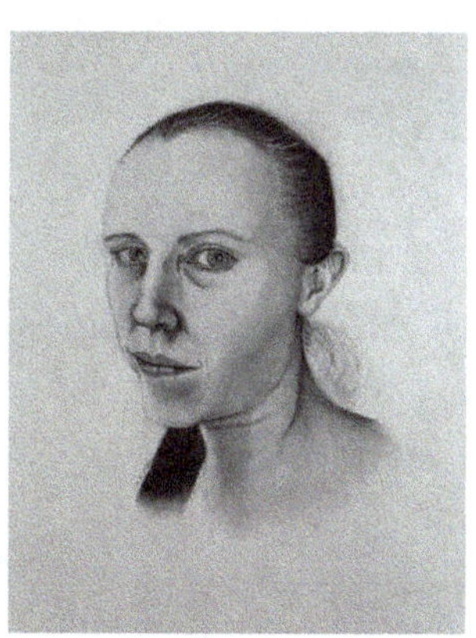

Sarah Merritt Ryan is a poet, blogger, and writer of memoir. She writes of her experiences with emotionally surviving serious mental illness, telling her unique story. Her poetry has been published in anthologies by Whispering Angels Books, Prolific Pulse Press, and PurpleStone Press.

Indy Samra

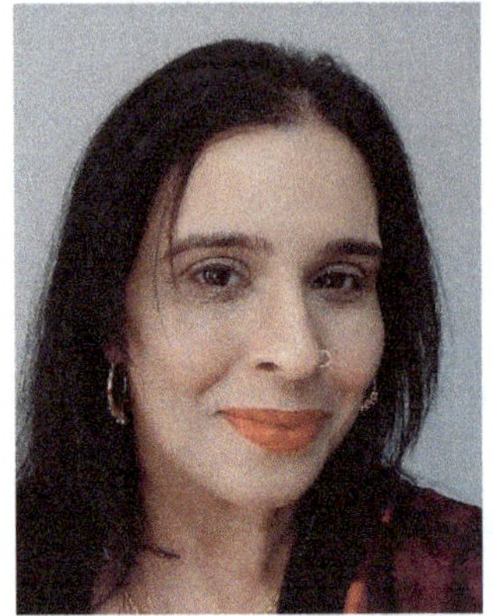

Indy Samra is a female author and Wellness facilitator. Mindfulness exercises, meditations, poetry, memoirs and children's and adult's short fictional stories are published in anthologies. She is inspired by the balance of her Punjabi heritage and being second generation British Asian. To find out more follow social media platforms Indy Essence.

Pratibha Savani

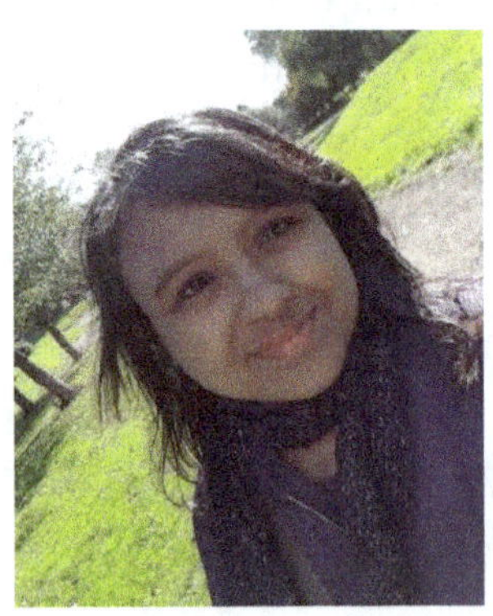

Pratibha Savani is a UK poet, artist, and author of 'Tangles + Knots'. Published in over fifty publications of various anthologies and magazines, she is a creative soul, inspired by the cosmos, nature, and spirituality. Pratibha likes to defy the rules with her inventive expressions on instagram and facebook as @pratibhapoetryart.

Shiela Denise Scott

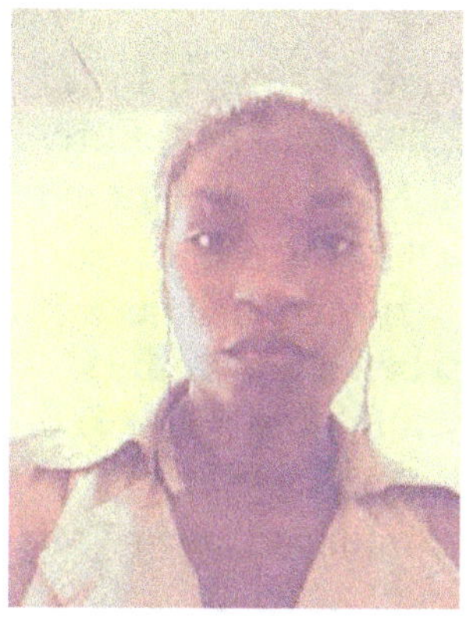

Shiela Denise Scott holds a Bachelor of Fine Arts degree in Creative Writing earned at Full Sail University and an Applied degree of Arts and Science in Digital Photography at Antonelli College. Her works, which include photographs, quotes, poems, and letters have been displayed in multiple magazines and anthologies. She loves to entertain the art connoisseur. Follow her on social media at Facebook, X, and Instagram.

Richa Dinesh Sharma

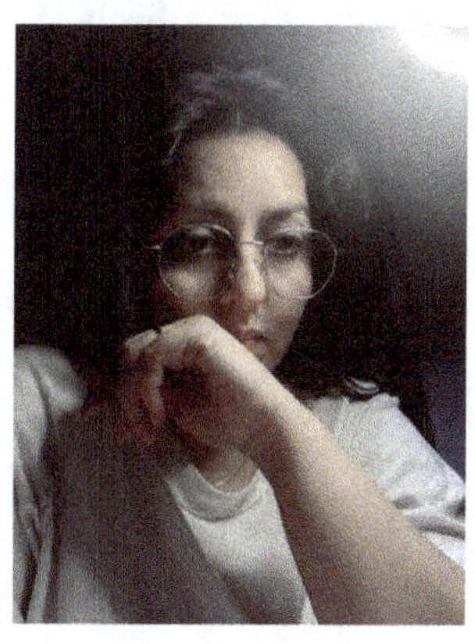

Richa Dinesh Sharma lives in Singapore with her husband, two human children and one furchild. Her poems have featured in FineLines quarterly issues, OpenDoor Poetry magazine, MockingHeart Review, Medium and several anthologies. She dabbles in Art when not writing or daydreaming. On Instagram @dryink_brush.

Anka Stanojčić

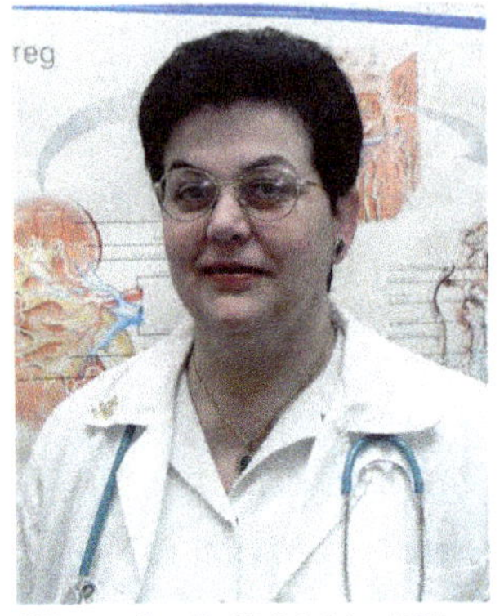

Anka Stanojčić was born in 1951 in Makarska. She spent her entire working life at KBC Zvezdara in Belgrade, as a specialist internist. She has been writing since her school days, when she was the editor of the youth newspaper "20. October" in Makarska. She published four books of poetry and short prose: "Waltz" (2009), "Rumba" (2011), "Tango" (2013) and "Blues" in 2017, as well as the novel "Čekam te na strani deset" (winner of the " Balkan Jeweler" and a candidate for the City of Belgrade Award, 2020), the poetry collection "Love of Tides and Tides" and the novella "Because of you Dadday" (2023). She published her works in literary magazines and periodicals. She is the winner of the third prize for a short story of the "Ivo Andrić" literary club in 2021. She is the editor of the magazine "Pobednik" of the Society of Writers of Belgrade. She worked as the secretary of the "Scena Crnjanski" literary club in 2010-2011. 2017-2022, then as the secretary of the "Society of Writers of Belgrade" 2017-2022, where she is now moderator and vice president.

Chanah Liora Wizenberg

Chanah Wizenberg's poems, stories, and articles have been published in several anthologies and magazines, including the Heron Clan, Vol 8, Reflections & Revelations, TAF Omnibus, Vol 2, Fines Lines, and Cary Magazine. She's a retired ballerina, pastry chef, and English teacher. In her free time Chanah swims and lifeguards at her local YMCA. She resides in Raleigh, North Carolina with her dog, Asha, and her cat, Marmalade.

Lisa Tomey-Zonneveld

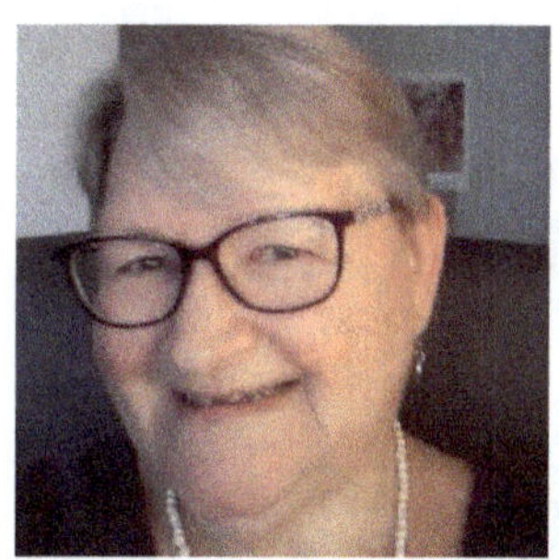

Lisa Tomey-Zonneveld is the founder and manager of Prolific Pulse Press LLC and a widely published poet and writer. She is the editor of numerous anthologies and is an editor for *Fine Lines Journal*. Tomey-Zonneveld has served as Poet Laureate of Garden of Neuro Institute and resides in North Carolina.

Creative Director:
Pratibha Savani

Pratibha Savani first began writing as a student struggling with eczema, releasing her debut book, 'Tangles + Knots' in October 2020. It uniquely combines her art and writing with mindfulness and wellbeing themes and was featured in the August 2021 'Garden of Neuro Poetry Book Club.' Her black and white art became the inspiration for the anthology series, "A Safe and Brave Space" by adding mindfulness colouring and has contributed towards all the anthologies as well as delivering the online art workshops and designing the book cover concept for Volume Two.

Pratibha became the Creative Director for Volume Three and has worked closely on the manuscript with Nanci Arvizu and Lisa Tomey-Zonneveld. She has enjoyed making creative decisions around the structure, layout, fonts, colours, editing and creating the journal pages, which has a subtle rainbow theme running throughout the anthology. She has also produced the artwork and designed the book cover reflecting the colours theme within Volume Three.

"Whenever I design or write something, I like the freedom to create without rules or restrictions and this is how new ideas and possibilities open up. The Garden of Neuro has been a life changing experience creatively. I have had the joy of meeting like-minded individuals who share a great passion for art and poetry, and I thank Lisa Tomey-Zonneveld for her continuous advice and support. I am truly grateful for this creative journey."

~ With Love Pratibha

From GoNI/P Director of Publishing: Nanci Arvizu

It has been a lifelong dream I didn't even know I was having, to be here, in the Garden of Neuro, with this global community of women, sharing our stories, and wisdom as we meet, collaborate, support, and celebrate each other, the highs and lows, and everything in between.

The transformation I have experienced because of my involvement in The Garden of Neuro Institute, is an exciting new chapter in my life, one I hope will continue for years.

The Garden has opened doors to people, places, and purposes I would have never known. Meeting Garden Founder Susan Brearley and experiencing her Garden Vision firsthand opened my mind to so many new possibilities, understandings and explorations.

No Mud, No Lotus. If you've been in the Garden, you may have heard this phrase. There is nourishment in the mud, and joy when its beauty blossoms.

This book, A Safe and Brave Space, Volume 3, and Volumes 1 and 2, are our collective Lotus. We've all been through some mud in our lives. And we're lucky when someone offers us help because they can see our struggle. After all, they have been there too.

Creating collaborative projects and communities around a shared vision to provide opportunities for women to become who they are meant to be, and to help the people we are meant to help; this is why we are all here. To be the Lotus seed, waiting in the mud means we may not be at our best right now. We just need a little more time to grow out of it.

The Mentor:
Lisa Tomey-Zonneveld

Lisa Tomey-Zonneveld has been the driving force behind this poetry project from the beginning. Without her at this table, these books, and the relationships they have formed, would not have happened.

What Lisa brings to these projects, besides her years of experience in her solo-prenurer business Prolific Pulse Press LLC, is her joy in sharing her wisdom. This is what the Garden is really about - helping the next woman in the ways that we can so she can achieve her goals faster. The sooner we get to where we are going, the sooner we can begin to plan for the next adventure. And, help, or be helped by those along the way.

Lisa embodies this philosophy with kindness, humor, and a generous helping of grace when necessary.

I would like to thank Lisa for all of her gentle guidance personally. The wisdom she has shared during the creation of all the Garden Anthologies, past, present, and future, will be remembered, honored, and celebrated with every volume.

Thank you Lisa

~ Nanci

Garden of Neuro Publishing

www.GardenofNeuroPublishing.com